Your Money's Worth

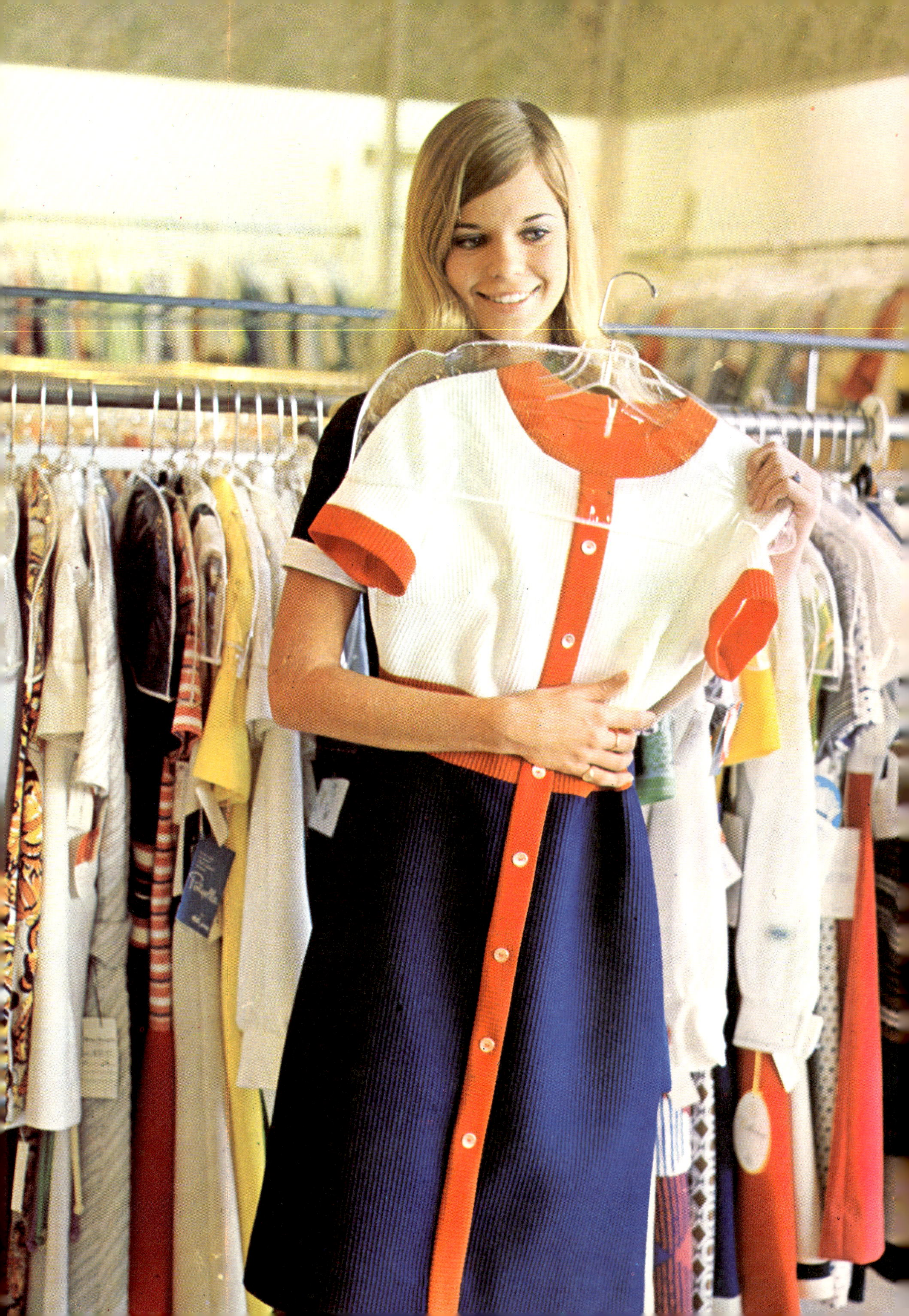

WOMAN ALIVE

Your Money's Worth

by Susan Allen

Aldus Books London

Series Coordinator: John Mason
Design Director: Guenther Radtke
Picture Editor: Peter Cook
Editor: Mitzi Bales
Research: Ann Fisher
Marian Pullen
Consultants: Beppie Harrison
Jo Sandilands

Copyright © 1973 Aldus Books
Limited, London

Library of Congress
Catalog No. 72-85024

Printed and bound in Yugoslavia by
Mladinska Knjiga, Ljubljana.

Contents

It takes a smart buyer to get value for money these days—and this book is designed to help you become one of the smart ones. Here are tips on how you can get more for your money when you buy. They cover almost everything you need, from everyday items such as food and clothing, through to big money expenses such as your car, your freezer —and your home. You will also find basic information on what you should know about credit, insurance, savings, and even investing—in language that talks to you as a woman. Grouped in a final section of the book is important information on education planning, Social Security benefits, and specific consumer traps to guard against. In all, this is a book that can be worth a lot to you in pointing out ways to make your dollar go farther.

	The Barter Business: Picture Essay	6
1	Managing Your Money	16
2	Buying For Every Day	27
3	Credit Buying	45
4	The Big Buy	54
5	Home Buying and Renting	82
6	Buying Life and Health Insurance	107
7	You Too Can Invest!	120
	Questions and Answers	129
	For Your Bookshelf	144

The Barter Business

Exchanging one thing for another has been a basic activity since two cavemen decided each preferred the other's meat, and traded.

Right: bartering is a basic language between people of different cultures. The fur traders of North America had to use the goods of civilization to bargain with the Indians.

Below: "money" is whatever people will accept in exchange for their goods. Here one of the sailors under Captain Cook is using a bottle to buy a lobster from a Maori man.

Below right: for thousands of years, long camel caravans moved across Asia, bringing its riches to Europe, and vice versa.

Right: in parts of the world bartering and money live side by side. In this Kenya market, you can pay in kind or with coins.

Below: in southern California the swap meet brings bartering up to date. You rent a spot, set up a table, and you're in business.

Below: the swap meets offer a choice of barter or buying—either way, what might have gone on your junk heap can become a treasured possession for somebody else!

7

The Evolution of Money

Money is the most portable form of wealth, and it has taken many shapes over the centuries. It can really be any object that is recognized as having a specific value.

Right: this boar's jaw from the New Hebrides has had the upper incisors removed to use for money for ritual payments or for bride prices.

Below: in ancient times they used lumps of salt (*sal* in Latin) to pay the wages, or "salary", of Roman soldiers. Obviously, a lazy or incompetent man wasn't worth his salt!

Below: wampum belts, made up of shell beads. The colors had differing values. Wampum beads were used in trade between Indians and colonists in the early days.

Right: men have used coins since the Lydians issued the top coin in the 7th century B.C. The others are "pieces of eight".

Above: the Chinese were probably the first to use paper money. Marco Polo reported seeing it used in the 13th century, and this picture illustrates the Khan and his mint.

Above: this pile of gold, silver, and bills adds up to $2½ million—but of course the real value of money depends on what it buys.

Keeping It Safe

However portable money might be, most people prefer not to carry too much of it around with them—banks were founded as strong, secure places in which to leave it.

Right: where there is money, there quickly are bills. This one is Babylonian, written in 3000 B.C., presenting a merchant's bill.

Below: the earliest banks were the strong-boxes of the moneylenders, who would agree to keep a customer's money safe.

Right: like most of us, she starts saving money first in a splendidly fat piggy bank, hearing the pennies jingling in and dreaming of great shining mounds piling up inside.

Right: the fascination of a bank, with its special sort of solemnity, was as enthralling to young Victorians as to our children today.

Above: all kinds of people rely on banking services today to help manage their money.
Below: traditional austerity is brightened with colorful checks issued by some banks.

Scarcity Value

What makes a thing valuable? Some objects gain value for their beauty, some for their function—and many things are valuable simply because there are so few of them around. Gold was the precious possession of generations of rich men because it is found only in limited quantities.

Right: gold bullion still retains a special appeal. People caught in desperate times of wild inflation or war often find that gold maintains its value best.

Below: for many wealthy people, possession of works of art like this masterpiece by Rembrandt represents far more than beauty —such works are enormous investments.

Above: there are stamp collectors and stamp collectors. The anonymous philatelist who now owns this treasure, the British Guiana One Cent stamp, paid almost $300,000 for it.

Right: two exquisite trinkets made by Peter Carl Faberge, the Russian goldsmith, who made imperial Easter eggs, like the one here, for the delight of the Russian royal family.

Above: the racehorse Nijinsky won so many races so magnificently that at his retirement he was valued at $5½ million.

Right: a spectacular diamond, worn here by Elizabeth Taylor. It is a pear-shaped stone, weighing 69.42 carats. When Richard Burton bought it in 1969, it cost $1,200,000.

Shopping Around

The pleasure and purpose of money is surely in spending it, and the world is full of tempting places where it can be spent. The supermarket is only one of a huge variety of ways to shop throughout the world.

Right: food shopping for the household has traditionally been the job for the housewife. Our trip to the supermarket is the latest of a long line of shopping customs.

Below: the Dye Bazaar in Marrakesh, Morocco, to western eyes an exotic and mysterious place where traders gather and local gossip is rife.

Above: waterborne shopkeepers rest on their oars in a floating market in Bangkok, Thailand. The graceful "shops" present a picturesque—as well as useful—scene.

Above: GUM, Moscow's famous department store. Kremlinologists have spent long hours analyzing its displays of consumer goods to discover Soviet economic developments.

Below: Macy's in New York, the world's biggest department store, has a floor space of 46.2 acres and over 11,000 employees.

Above: and of course you need not go to the store yourself. Nationwide, the stores will come to you, in the glossy, tempting catalogs of the country's mail-order firms.

15

Managing Your Money
1

Do you wonder how the Wilsons could spend a month in Puerto Rico last summer? Or how the Bryants can afford dinner-and-a-show so often? You know they have about the same income and expenses as you, but they seem to manage so much better.

Management is the key. Most people cringe at the words "money management". They think of giant corporations, and high finance, and professional accountants. Yet managing money is not only essential to your family's well-being; it is also part of the art of living. For, if you use the money you have to best advantage, you can do more to create the kind of lifestyle you want.

Anyone can get some know-how about using money more wisely. With a little effort, you can chase the terror out of such subjects as interest rates, credit and collateral, life insurance premiums, and house closing charges. Then, with your new-found knowledge, you may find yourself handling family finances so well that there's something left for life's wonderful extras.

Luckily, getting what you want for yourself and your family does not necessarily depend on how much you or your husband makes. At every level of yearly income—all the way from $6,500 to $40,000—you can find families that manage beautifully and those that are miserable. Some families making $25,000 a year or more own $60,000 homes and two cars, but have trouble meeting their simple expenses. Farther down on the scale, there are families like the Youngs. Peter, a foreman in a small factory, earns $10,000. Because of Sally's good management, the Youngs are buying their own home, are planning to send their children to college, and

Coping with the problems of expenses and income is a necessary part of the job of running a family—and seldom the favorite task. But making a thoughtful effort to rationalize your approach to your money can make the whole business far more pleasant, as well as making your dollars work harder for you.

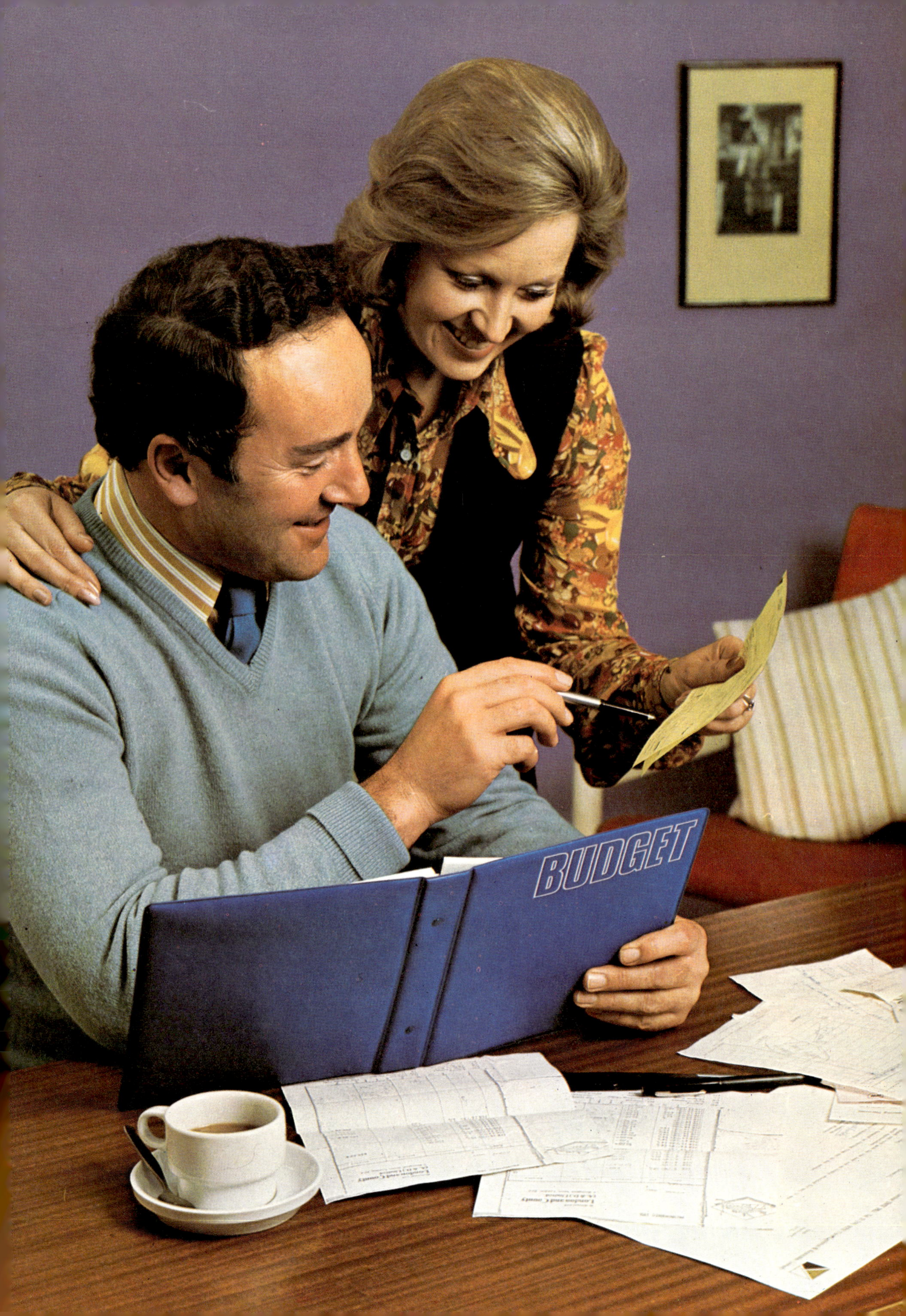
BUDGET

have laid a foundation for a secure retirement.

Sally Young knows that good management does not simply mean staying out of debt. It means getting the most for your money, and stretching every dollar as far as it will go. When you begin shopping more shrewdly, you'll wonder why you were ever content to pay $1 for an item you can get for less.

It takes a lot of planning—and even more of self-discipline—to shop and spend wisely. Most of your savings will be on the small side, too. But pennies can mount up to many dollars for a car, a vacation, or retirement security in the future. Besides, the hard work that goes into forming good spending habits has a reward beyond simply savings: it can give you great pleasure and satisfaction in knowing you're making money your servant rather than your master.

Budgeting is Good Planning
Design your family budget to make life easier, and to let you spend more money on the things you most need and want—or to save more money if that is a goal. When it begins to seem like a prison, it should be changed. Anyway, most people can't stick to formal budgets—that is, making an exact monthly allotment for all expenditure, based on present income and expected expenses. No matter how you plan or forecast for the future, something unexpected crops up. It could be anything from a change of jobs, to a flat tire, to a small legacy from Uncle Bill. Suddenly you have more or less money than you had figured on, and, happily or unhappily, your budget goes out the window. A strict, down-to-the-penny budget is unrealistic. Your written budget should be a general plan for living your life, not a forecast of how you spend every dollar. Make sure the budget fits in with the whole picture, and allows you to meet your fixed expenses with something left over.

Counselors suggest that all members of your family take part in budget planning—even the children—and that each person be given an allowance with no strings attached, no matter how small. Your budget can cover

Below left and right: this young couple finds it hard to make ends meet even with an above-average income. A high mortgage and heavy taxes on their attractive home are a big part of their expenses. But rising costs all along the line make it more important than ever for all to learn —and practice—good money management.

Below right: a family with a $10,000 annual income in 1949 could live as well as a family earning $18,960 today. It would take $48,400 in 1973 to equal a 1949 income of $25,000, and a staggering $100,450 now to buy what you could for $50,000 in 1949. These figures show how the purchasing power of the dollar has decreased over the last 24 years.

Dollars Buy Less Today

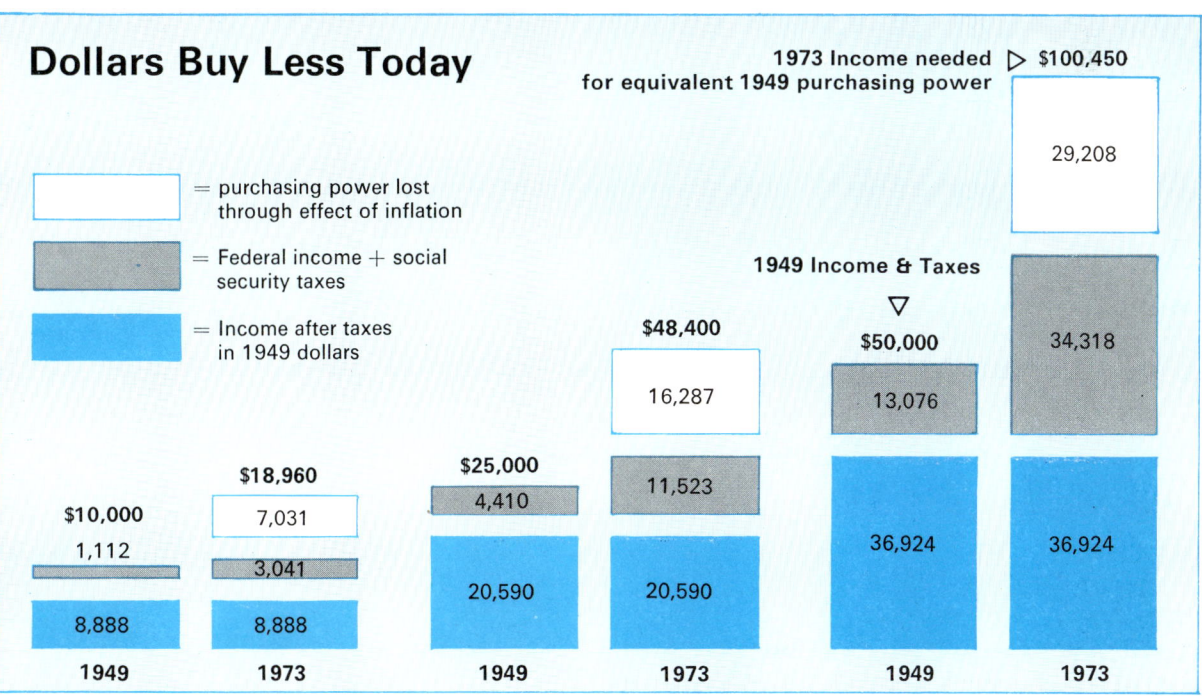

1973 Income needed ▷ $100,450
for equivalent 1949 purchasing power

☐ = purchasing power lost through effect of inflation

▨ = Federal income + social security taxes

▮ = Income after taxes in 1949 dollars

29,208

1949 Income & Taxes ▽

$48,400

$50,000

34,318

16,287

13,076

$18,960

$25,000

11,523

$10,000

7,031

4,410

1,112

3,041

36,924

36,924

20,590

20,590

8,888

8,888

| 1949 | 1973 | 1949 | 1973 | 1949 | 1973 |

19

any period, but most families find that a year is the most convenient. In making your budget, figure out how much income you can expect during the budget period. Start with your and your husband's take-home pay, and add whatever else is appropriate, such as interest on bank accounts, or dividends on stocks. If you can swing it, it's best to let interest and dividends accumulate. Then you get interest on the interest, and you can reinvest the dividends.

The next step is establishing how much you will spend during this period—and this is where most budgets go wrong. It is easy to predict fixed expenses, like rent or mortgage payments, utilities, insurance premiums, and installment payments. It is not much harder to estimate grocery and entertainment costs. But it may be impossible to estimate medical care, and it's a good idea to keep some cash aside for that purpose alone. To help you estimate the less fixed items, look back through old check books, bills, or any other record you can find, and get an idea of what you spent on them in the past. In addition to regular expenses, add in large seasonal expenses, such as vacations, and—if you pay them directly—income and property taxes. Last, set down the amount you are saving for long-term goals. If the total of your expenses is the same, or close to, your estimated income, consider your budget balanced. If expenses are much more than income, you'll have to cut somewhere. Perhaps adjusting can be as simple as buying cheaper cuts of meat, or using the car less often for short trips. Maybe it will have to be a stronger measure, such as making your own clothes.

Do you worry that you spend too much on movies and clothes, even though you stay pretty well within your income? Or do you feel guilty about not giving more to charity?

The family paycheck is spent for a wide variety of things: some, like housing, food, and taxes, are compulsory for everyone. Others, like recreation, are more variable. The way each family chooses to spend its money expresses the family's personality —and its priorities in creating its chosen lifestyle.

If so, it might help to know how your spending compares with that of other American families. The following table from the US Bureau of Labor Statistics will give you something of a picture. It is based on an average city worker's budget for a family of four: a husband, a nonworking wife, a son of 13, and a daughter of 8. Their annual income is $10,970.

Food.............................$2532 (23.1%)
Housing........................$2638 (24.0%)
Transportation...............$ 964 (8.8%)
Personal taxes...............$1784 (16.3%)
Medical care..................$ 612 (5.6%)
Miscellaneous (recreation, alcoholic beverages, tobacco, etc.)...................$ 684 (6.2%)
Clothing, personal care.....$1196 (10.9%)
Gifts, contributions, etc. ...$ 560 (5.1%)

Of course, you may have a higher or lower income than this model family, which was used by a government agency for illustrative purposes. You may think that 23.1 per cent is too high for food, or 10.9 per cent too low for clothing. Remember, though, that these statistics are based on wide investigation of family living costs. If you stop to figure out what you spend on the listed items over the year, you might be surprised to find that it comes close to the *percentages* shown.

The Checking Account for You

You love your checking account for its convenience, so you may never have thought about its cost. Yet you could save money by figuring out the best kind of account for your family needs.

The two basic types of checking accounts are "regular" and "special". A regular account requires you to keep a minimum balance, usually of $200 to $500. You pay a service charge based on the amount of money you keep in the account, how many checks you write, and the number of deposits you make. Charges vary from bank to bank, depending on individual formulas for calculating them. One of the first things to do, then, is to find out your bank's method of arriving at its charges. Another bank might charge less in your particular case. The regular account is generally an advantage for bigger depositors, and a disadvantage for those of us whose balance dwindles to $5 at the end of the month.

For a special checking account, you are charged about 15 cents for each check written, and a monthly service fee of about $1, no matter how high or low your balance. It won't be hard for you to figure out which account is cheaper for you. Tabulate the number of checks you write each month, and take note of the monthly balance. If you use a good number of checks, and don't want to cut down, and if you can maintain the required balance with it all, the regular account will probably be more economical.

Keep in mind that checks, regular or special, cost money to use. You can make an easy saving by writing as few checks as possible. Be especially careful not to leave yourself completely cashless, so that you have to write checks for many small items—laundry, dry cleaning, and pocket money, for example. If you cut the number of checks you use from 15 to 6 in a month, you'll save $10.80 a year.

Naturally, you should keep an accurate record of the money in your account. In the first place, this is insurance against having checks bounce—and paying extra service fees for doing so. Secondly, accurate records are invaluable in working out tax deductions. A tip on canceled checks: keep the ones for tax and insurance payments for at least six years. That is how long the Internal Revenue can go back into your financial records.

Which Bank For Your Savings?
Your Grandma may have chosen between a bank or an old sock to keep her savings in. Today, the choice is often between kinds of banks—and it's important to know what difference your choice could mean.

The institutions providing savings accounts are commercial banks, savings banks, savings and loan associations (sometimes called savings and loan companies, cooperative banks, or homestead associations), and mutual savings banks. Credit unions are becoming more popular for savings, but membership requirements limit their general use. The main question to ask yourself is, "Which pays the highest interest?" In some states, savings banks are allowed to pay higher interest than commercial banks, but laws vary from state to state. Generally speaking, however, savings and loan associations, mutual savings banks, and credit unions pay the highest rates. By reading newspaper ads and the leaflets put out by various savings institutions, you can easily learn which type offers the most interest. You might watch particularly for the ads of savings and loan associations in California, Nevada, and Alaska. They are noted for their high interest rates—one-

Left: the conveniences offered by banking services can follow you around the world. Your traveler's checks can be used almost anywhere, saving the dangers of carrying large amounts of cash around with you.

Right: using a checking account sensibly means keeping a regular record of where you stand, and checking that against the bank statements.

fourth to one-half per cent higher than elsewhere—and often advertise in far-flung places for bank-by-mail business. You must realize, of course, that your money is not as readily available as it is in a local bank, and that there might be complications on inheritance in case of death.

It's worth your while to look for the highest interest rate because, in time, an extra 1 per cent can mean a lot. For a simple example, let's take $1000 and keep it in the bank for five years. At 4 per cent interest compounded quarterly, your money will have earned $220.19 in five years. At 5 per cent interest compounded quarterly, it would have earned $282.04 in interest. Perhaps this doesn't look like so much on $1000, but suppose your account grows by $1000 each year. You can see, then, how that extra 1 per cent can gradually mount up.

As you compare the various savings institutions, you will notice that most commercial banks compound your interest either quarterly or semiannually, while an increasing number of savings banks in large urban areas compound daily. Compounding interest daily gives you an extra 0.2 per cent a year. It's not much, but it can add up. The secret of success in making compounding work harder for you is to choose a bank that offers a grace period. This means that if you deposit money up to the tenth of the month, or another given day, you get interest on it as though you had put it in on the first of the month. Bonus interest also increases your savings faster. This means a bank pays an extra percentage on money left in your account for a full interest period.

How Savings Dollars Grow

$40,000	
$35,000	**$36,801**
$30,000	
$25,000	Amount added by compound interest
$20,000	Deposited in a savings account at 5½% interest compounded semiannually — **$21,840**
$15,000	
$10,000	Deposited in "the mattress"
$5,000	
years	5 10 15 20

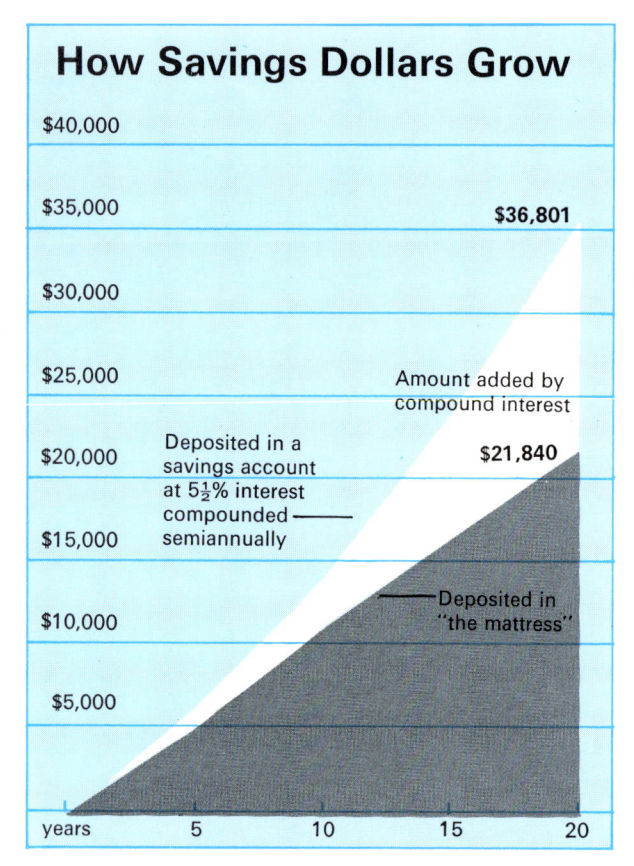

Regular savings deposited in a savings account will steadily increase, unlike a nest egg tucked away in the dubious safety of the mattress. If you saved $3 every day, you would have about $36,801 after 20 years. This is because even a small amount increases rapidly when interest is paid on interest. If you have no interest coming on your $3 daily savings, you would have only a little more than half as much in 20 years' time—about $21,840.

You will also find that many banks offer higher interest on long-term accounts, sometimes called CD accounts (for Certificates of Deposit). A long-term account involves making a minimum deposit, usually $500, and leaving it untouched for a specified period. Ninety days is the shortest, but two years or longer is more usual. These conditions give the bank the advantage of knowing just how long it can use your money for its own investments, and permits it to guarantee the interest rate for the stated period, no matter what happens to the bank's general interest rates. If you withdraw your money before the agreed time, you must pay a penalty, which is generally the loss of the last 90 days of extra interest.

Banking institutions are so well protected these days that it is virtually unnecessary to check on their credentials before you do business with them. However, to reassure yourself, look for a Federal Deposit Insurance Corporation (FDIC) notice in banks, and a Federal Savings and Loan Insurance Corporation (FSLIC) announcement in savings and loan associations. These government insurance programs protect your personal funds up to $15,000 per depositor. If there is no FDIC or FSLIC sign, ask if there is a state insurance program to which the institution subscribes.

Tips on How to Save
Unless you are a born gambler, you are probably already saving, or planning to in the near future. Here are a few tricks to make saving less painful.

For the next month or two, count the money in your purse each time you leave the house. Count it again when you return, and note down what you spent—even if you charged it—and what you spent it on. Keep this information in a notebook, and look it over from time to time. You'll probably discover that dollars have been frittered away for things you neither wanted or needed. These diverted dollars should be channeled into savings.

Many employers will deposit pay checks directly into a bank account on request. You may decide that this is the easiest way to help you save. All that cash is put where it can't tempt you, and having to write a check may slow down your spending for the little things. You could also ask your bank to withdraw $5 from your checking account, and deposit it in your savings account each week. It's the same as if you were making a regular payday deposit, but much surer.

By now, hopefully, you feel easier about the whole idea of good money management on the family level. In the next chapters, you will find basic and detailed information to help you even further. So, let's next tackle the problem of everyday spending for the essentials: food and clothing.

Right: this diagram shows where most Americans choose to put their savings—and it's clear that commercial banks are out in front as the favorite. Savings and loan associations are a close second.

Below: even though commercial banks pay the lowest interest rates, they remain popular because of their other convenient services. These include checking accounts, personal loans, and mortgages.

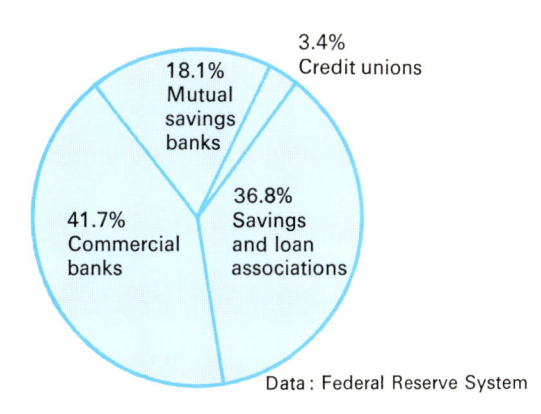

3.4% Credit unions
18.1% Mutual savings banks
41.7% Commercial banks
36.8% Savings and loan associations

Data: Federal Reserve System

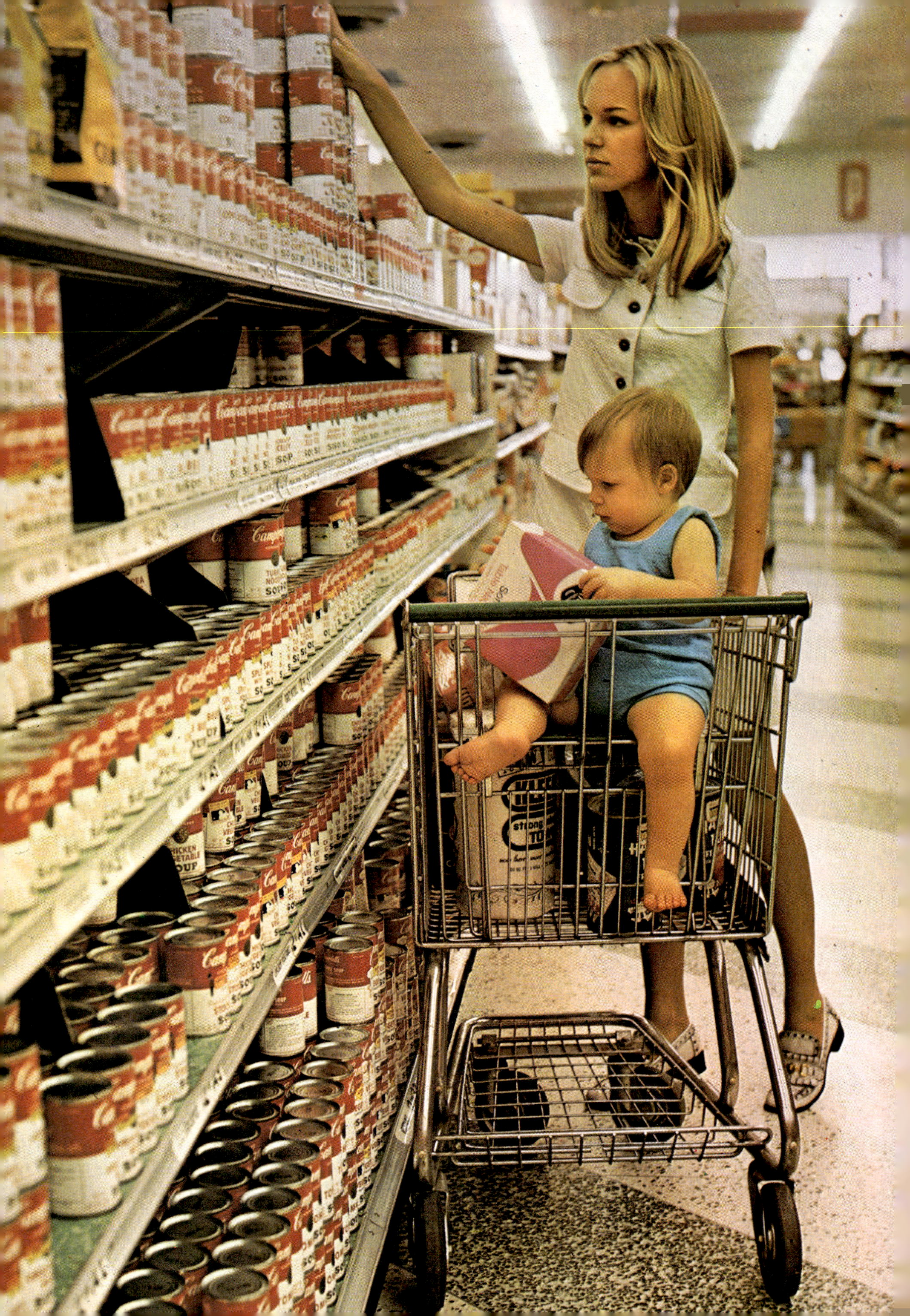
Campbell's
CHICKEN VEGETABLE SOUP

Buying for Every Day
2

What you eat and what you wear are two of the most important aspects of your whole lifestyle. Beware general statistics on the amounts others spend on food and clothing. They are not always a suitable guide for you. Some families simply won't stand for certain food economies. Other families have job and entertainment demands that create certain clothing requirements. No one wants to take the joy out of eating or the pride out of dressing well. Nonetheless, there are some principles of buying that can help you cut your food and clothing costs without starving your family, or looking as if you dressed in cast-offs.

After housing, food usually accounts for the biggest chunk of the family budget. Of course, if your family insists on generous portions of roast beef and rich desserts these days, your food costs will soar. Almost every family could practice a little control on food buying without a bit of sacrifice on nutrition, tastiness, and enjoyment of what they eat.

It isn't easy, but you can do it if you want to—and there are some general rules that can help. For example, plan your menus for the week, and shop according to that plan. In this way, you can mix cheaper meals among the more expensive ones, so that you don't wind up at the end of the week or month on a steady diet of macaroni and cheese. Nothing takes the pleasure out of saving as quickly as having the family complain, "Ugh, not *that* again."

Another guide to painless savings is to learn what the US Department of Agriculture (USDA) grades mean—and to learn how to use them to advantage. The USDA has put out a booklet that explains it all, and you might want to have a copy for handy reference. The title is *How to Use USDA Grades in Buying Food*. It is available for 15 cents if you write to: Superintendent of Documents, Government Printing Office, Washington, D.C. 20402. Ask for Department of Agriculture publication "HG 196".

Unfortunately, many canned and packaged foods are not marked with USDA grades, although they may have been processed in accordance with grading standards. This means you must take greater care in buying processed foods.

Saving on Meat

Meat is undoubtedly the biggest single item on your shopping list. Most American families spend nearly 30 cents of every grocery dollar on red meat—which means beef, lamb, or pork. The most important thing to know about saving on meat is that every cut of the same kind of meat has virtually the same nutritional value, even though the cheaper cuts have more bone, gristle, and inedible fat. There is more waste on cheap cuts, then, but they don't shortchange your family on healthful food.

Here is where USDA grades can help you. It is usually only beef that is clearly marked in retail stores, but, happily, it is savings on beef that can cut meat bills the most. Beef grades tell you how tender, juicy, and

It's easy to rush around a familiar supermarket filling the cart with the same things you always get, but you may be spending money you could save by checking on price differences between brands, making sure that the week's specials are bargains for you, and by buying only what's on your list.

With the prices of the most ordinary foods rising year after year, most housewives find themselves doing extremely careful bargain shopping.

Far right: between 1940 and 1973, prices of 9 common foods have risen steadily to new highs.

flavorful the meat will be. *Choice* is the highest grade you'll usually find at retail. Choice beef is well marbleized—that is, it has firm white fat distributed throughout the lean—and is also coated with thick creamy fat. This is what gives tenderness and taste when meat is broiled or roasted. Beef graded *Good*, the only other grade you're likely to see in the supermarket, is quite lean and fairly tender. If you can find it, good grade beef offers the best quality at a moderate price.

If you take a little special care in cooking, you can get both flavor and tenderness out of cheap cuts. Use tenderizer on a chuck steak and you can challenge anyone to tell it from sirloin. Try bottom round for a pot roast, cook it slowly with seasoning and vegetables—and listen to the lip-smacking pleasure of the family. A blade pot roast is even cheaper.

Keep in mind that when you figure meat costs, you must do it on a per serving basis. Figuring by the pound will not take waste or bone into account. A pound of ground beef, for example, yields about four servings, and a pound of rolled rib roast only three. This makes ground beef a double money-saver.

Another way of reducing food costs is to serve organ meats such as liver, heart, tripe, brains, and tongue. Many Americans are put off by them, though they are eaten the world over with relish. There are many flavorful ways to prepare them, and their nutritional value is as high—often higher—as the animal's flesh.

If your family already likes calf's liver, introduce cheaper beef liver next. Braised or casseroled—in fact, any way except broiled—beef liver is hard to tell from calf's. For still greater savings, try pork liver. The somewhat stronger taste can be modified by cooking pork liver the Italian or Spanish way, with onions and green peppers.

Chicken is a good source of protein that is lower in price than meat. It can be prepared in many tasty ways, and is a popular food with most people. For a change, try the old-fashioned method of stewing or fricaseeing chicken with dumplings, or the French way of long cooking with wine. In such ways you can turn out delicious meals with rather tough stewing chickens, which are older birds. They cost up to 15 cents less than the young—and more tender—broilers or fryers.

If you buy whole birds and cut them up yourself at home, you can save from 2 to 10 cents a pound. Another economy is to buy only the wings, which are cheap. Use whole

How Inflation Hits Food Costs

wings for making stock, or strip the meat from large wings for use in salad.

Make turkey a treat on *any* Thursday of the year, and you'll make real savings on meat. Pound for pound of useable meat, turkey is always a good buy. It's an even better buy out of the Thanksgiving and Christmas holiday seasons when prices rise due to increased demand.

Milk

Next to meat, milk is probably what you spend most of your food money on—and for good reason. Milk is often called "the perfect food" because of its high nutritional value, and it should be part of the family's daily diet. In these days of constantly rising milk prices, however, some economy is called for.

The biggest savings on milk come by using nonfat dry milk, which gives you all the proteins, vitamins, and minerals of whole milk without the butterfat. The missing butterfat makes it a boon to weight watchers, but many milk drinkers don't like the taste. If your family is choosy that way, you can still take advantage of the economy of nonfat dry milk in other ways. Use reconstituted powdered milk instead of whole milk in soups, omelettes, cakes and cookies, custards, and puddings—in fact, in almost any recipe calling for milk.

To improve the flavor for drinking, mix powdered milk the night before. Also try mixing part skim milk liquid with whole milk—first in a small amount, then perhaps in increasing amounts, if the family bears with it.

Two other tips on milk savings: save from 2 to 4 cents per quart by cutting out home delivery; and get half-gallon containers to save another 2 cents per quart. If you can find a dealer who sells milk by the gallon, your savings by such bulk purchases will go up even more.

Sanity in the Supermarket
The average supermarket is stocked with 8000 to 10,000 different items in a huge number of shapes and sizes, most with eye-catching packaging and labels. Separating the good values from the money-wasting buys is no mean task, but it is made easier with a shopping list you have prepared and thought out in advance.

Good shoppers guard against being fooled by the vast number of shapes and sizes of processed foods. To the careless shopper, the biggest box or can always contains the most of anything—detergent, green beans, cereal, or whatever—or the same size always contains the same amount. This is not the case, and, unless you make a habit of reading labels with keen attention, it's easy to be caught off base.

Most supermarkets show the price per pound, although they are required to do so by law only in New York, Connecticut, Rhode Island, Vermont, Maryland, and the city of Seattle. Some stores, mainly in the southeast, quote price per ounce. Both methods help make it easier for you to figure out the best buy, but you must still take care.

Beware of labels such as "economy size" and "jumbo size". The US Food and Drug Administration (FDA) recently seized thousands of jars of a well-known instant coffee whose label read "giant economy size". Each jar weighed 10 ounces, and cost $1.44 or 14.4 cents per ounce. The "regular size" jar of this same coffee was actually cheaper.

Left: you will find it's worth taking the time to talk to the butcher about cheaper cuts of meat you might be able to use. If you don't see a butcher on duty at the supermarket meat counter, you can ring a bell that calls him to the front; and if you choose a time when there is no rush, most butchers will be pleased to discuss meat selection with you.

Right: the great variety of cuts of beef are shown on this chart. Some are much more expensive than others because of taste and texture, but all can be cooked in a way to make them appetizing.

Beef Cuts and How to Cook Them

Ground Beef Roast or Broil	**Heel of Round** Braise or Simmer	**Round Steak** Braise	**Top Round** Braise	**Bottom Round** Braise
Hind Shank Soup or Simmer	**Rolled Rump** Braise or Roast	**Rump Roast** Braise or Roast	**Rolled Flank** Braise	
Flank Stew Stew	**Sirloin Steak** Broil or Panbroil	**Pin Bone Sirloin Steak** Broil or Panbroil	**Flank Steak** Braise	**Flank Steak Fillets** Braise
Porterhouse Steak Broil or Panbroil	**T Bone Steak** Broil or Panbroil	**Club Steak** Broil or Panbroil	**Plate Boiling Beef** Simmer or Braise	**Rolled Plate** Simmer or Braise
Short Ribs Simmer or Braise	**Standing Rib Roast** Roast	**Rolled Rib Roast** Roast	**Rib Steak** Broil	**Beef Brisket** Simmer
Corned Beef Simmer	**Blade Steak** Braise	**Blade Pot Roast** Braise	**Knuckle Bone** Soup or Braise	
Cross Cut Fore Shank Soup or Braise	**Triangle Pot Roast** Braise	**Boneless Chuck Pot Roast** Braise	**Shoulder Fillet** Braise	**English Cut** Braise
Arm Pot Roast Braise	**Arm Steak** Braise	**Rolled Neck** Braise or Stew	**Boneless Neck** Braise or Stew	

Food Buying Tips

Almost everybody has a stock of old wives' tales and superstitions about food: here's a crop of facts that can give you some help in stretching your food-buying dollar considerably further.

CHEESE

▶ Mild cheeses are lower in price than sharp ones, which must be aged longer.

▶ Most expensive least nutritional are processed cheeses, with fillers, in fancy jars.

▶ Buy grating cheese in a chunk and grate it yourself; also grate any cheese that has become hard before being used up.

▶ Slice it yourself; you pay extra for already sliced cheese.

▶ To store for better keeping, wrap cheese in foil, waxed paper, or cloth dampened with vinegar.

EGGS

▶ *Grade* is a government standard of quality; Grade AA is the best, but also the most expensive.

▶ Use cheaper Grade A instead of Grade AA for frying and boiling; the difference in taste and texture is slight.

▶ Use the cheapest Grade B for general cooking and baking; the quality is good, but thinner whites and runnier yolks make Grade B eggs spread more in frying or boiling.

▶ Buy by *size* to save money too; medium and small eggs are usually better buys than large in late summer and fall, large ones are the better buy in spring.

▶ White and brown shell eggs are of equal nutritional value; don't pay extra for shell color.

▶ Buy only from a refrigerated case, and never accept cracked eggs.

BUTTER AND MARGARINE

▶ Whipped butter is expensive; if you prefer it, whip it yourself in an electric mixer.

▶ Salted butter is cheaper than unsalted.

▶ Take only the amount of butter you need each time from the refrigerator; otherwise, part of it might go rancid.

▶ Margarine has the same food value as butter, and is cheaper.

▶ All margarine must meet federal standards for fat and Vitamin A content; therefore, the cheapest brand should be all right.

▶ Even if you prefer butter for the table, use margarine for general cooking and baking; mixing part butter and part margarine for non-table use is still something of a savings.

FRESH FRUITS AND VEGETABLES

▶ Buy both in season for best price.

▶ Buy both only in amounts you will use up quickly; pears, peaches, and avocadoes especially are best when fully ripe.

▶ Smaller size fruit is often cheaper; it's also a better buy for children.

▶ It's no savings to get vegetables cheaper because of some decay; a few extra pennies for products in good condition is a good investment.

▶ Buy fruit and vegetables loose so that you can pick out your own, when possible; you're more likely to get unspoiled ones.

▶ Thin-skinned oranges give more juice than thick-skinned ones; green color is not a sign of being unripe, because oranges are dyed.

CANNED GOODS

▶ Slices, chunks, and halves of fruits and vegetables are cheaper than whole ones.

▶ Private brands of supermarket chains are usually cheaper, and of good quality.

▶ Heavy syrup adds to the cost of canned fruit, it's also sweeter and more fattening.

▶ Don't buy cans that show signs of leakage, or bulge at the ends; dents are harmless unless the metal has been pierced.

CEREALS

▶ Sweetened cereals cost more; add sugar yourself and save.

▶ It's cheaper to buy several large boxes of different kinds than one package containing single portions of different varieties.

▶ Cooked cereals are cheaper than ready-to-serve ones.

▶ "Gifts" with box tops are no bargain; they cost the price of the cereal at least, and usually a bit more, but the gift is seldom of good quality.

One-stop shopping in a supermarket is a great convenience to most of us—but a supermarket is a business, not a charity, and all those attractive displays—and even the arrangement of the store—are designed mainly to persuade you to spend more money. The sensible shopper enjoys the convenience, evaluates the specials on display, takes the opportunity to look at new products, and then is careful to buy only the things she needs.

It weighed six ounces, and cost 75 cents, or 12.5 cents per ounce. It is also often a trick to label something "10 cents off". Unless the original price is stated, you have no way of being sure that a cut was made at all. A recent FDA regulation is designed to put a stop to these kinds of deceptive labels. It's hard to police government regulations in this vast country, however, so you have to watch for continuing abuse on labeling.

You Pay Too Much for Convenience
As a rule of thumb, it is best to stay away from convenience foods. Frozen dinners, vegetables in butter sauce, prepared puddings, sliced cheese, and a host of other foods that have been partially or wholly prepared for you by the manufacturer, all cost dearly. Take sliced cheese. You actually pay 24 to 48 cents more per pound for it than for the same cheese unsliced. According to Sidney Mar-

golius in his carefully documented book *The Great American Food Hoax,* frozen dinners tend to cost two to two-and-a-half times as much as the equivalent home-prepared versions. This might be worth it sometimes if frozen dinners had solid nutritional value—but they don't. They are often adulterated with starch sauces, breading, and thickening. Some prepared foods cost six to seven times more than the homemade product.

Many studies have been made on the cost of convenience foods. One by the New York State Cooperative Extension Service came up with these comparative per-serving prices on potatoes: fresh, 2 cents; canned 4 cents; instant mashed, 4 cents; frozen French fried, 6 cents; frozen fried puffs, 7 cents; and frozen, stuffed, baked, and topped with cheese, 19 cents.

To determine which convenience foods can save you money—and there are a number of them—figure out what one homemade serving costs, and compare it to the one-serving cost of the prepared variety. One convenience food that can save you money if you do careful comparison shopping is canned ham, because most canned ham has no bone and less fat than the butt ends in the meat case. Imported canned hams are generally a better buy than domestic ones because many US-packed hams have had water pumped into them.

The USDA publishes an extensive list of the convenience foods that are cheaper than their home-prepared versions. Among these are canned frozen juice concentrates (this leads most lists); frozen or canned spinach, green beans, and peas; canned beets, cut corn, cherries, spaghetti, and chicken chow mein. These foods are bargains partly because there is no waste. In his book *The Consumer's Guide to Better Buying,* Sidney Margolius names canned tomatoes, apple sauce, and grapefruit sections as other economical convenience foods. He also defends cake mixes, saying they save the housewife "half or more of preparation time at small extra cost."

Don't do your food shopping when you

35

are hungry. Experiments have shown that hungry shoppers spend 9 to 17 per cent more than their well-fed sisters. So don't delay your noon meal to rush to the supermarket. You're likely to overspend out of sheer appetite, and come home with bags of goodies you don't really need.

Check up on seasonal good buys before you make up your shopping list. Most newspapers and radio stations carry reports on the cheaper seasonal foods, as issued by the USDA.

Finally, make, and stick to, that important shopping list. If liquor is one of the items on that list, and you don't have to shop at a state liquor store, try to find a shop that sells its own private brands. Such private brands are cheaper, though often of equal quality with, advertised brands. In any case, most liquor tastes all right when used with mixers or in punch.

How to Save Big
If you are willing to go into saving food money in a big way, there is one more idea that might help—a co-op. Shoppers who have organized themselves into co-ops bypass the retailers, and go directly to the wholesaler. All you need to start one are enough people to buy bulk, a spirit of co-operation, and a station wagon or small truck to pick up and deliver the foods to co-op members. It involves a lot of hard work, careful planning, and group discipline according to those who have done it; but the savings that can be realized may make a co-op well worth the effort.

Dressing Well at Less Cost
Sally Woods was the undisputed "best dressed" in the neighborhood. Moreover, her whole family was a match for her. Everyone thought she spent a fortune on clothes, but the Woods' didn't seem to stint on food, or entertainment, or their house, or anything noticeable.

The truth is, Sally was a careful wardrobe planner. She bought winter coats only in the preseason or after-Christmas sales, and stocked up in quantity on hosiery, underwear, and socks during sales. In fact, almost every item of clothing was bought in sales. In addition, Sally stuck to simple lines, basic colors, and top quality products. Therefore her clothing wore well and long without ever looking last-yearish. She expressed her individual fashion flair by indulging in some of the current fads in accessories and extras, which made her whole outfit look up-to-the-minute—and she had some of her clothing allowance left for such things because of her overall planning.

Does it sound too dull and tiresome? Do you feel you must have that new smock top or wet-look raincoat the first day it appears in the store? Then you can hardly expect to be one of the Sally Woods of the world—looking like a million dollars on a moderate budget. If you want to try, though, the following suggestions will help you.

Something to keep in mind when you plan your wardrobe are the versatile transitional cottons—now, of course, generally combined with synthetics. Such dresses and separates are wearable for three seasons of the year. The sleeveless or short-sleeved dress with matching jacket is another wardrobe stretcher that stays long in fashion.

The handy diagram on page 41 will show you what to look for to make sure of good workmanship in the clothing you buy. A few basic rules: beware of crooked or puckering seams and dangling threads; look for sturdy buttons and closely bound, even buttonholes; make sure hems are at least 2 inches deep; check for reinforcements at pockets and stress points, such as placket

---

Americans are spoiled by the easy year-round availability of fruit and vegetables, and it is easy to get accustomed to planning meals without thinking about what's in season at the time. But it only takes a minute's thought to realize that if you are buying California lettuce in Boston, part of what you are paying for is freight! This chart shows approximate nationwide availability for an average year—yellow means that the products are in good supply, orange indicates a fair supply, and red, a small supply. Be a smart shopper, and plan to use what's produced locally in its season: you're bound to save money.

When Fruit is in Season

	January	February	March	April	May	June	July	August	September	October	November	December
Apples	●	●	●	●	●	●	●	●	●	●	●	●
Apricots					●	●	●	●				
Avocados	●	●	●	●	●	●	●	●	●	●	●	●
Bananas	●	●	●	●	●	●	●	●	●	●	●	●
Blueberries					●	●	●	●	●			
Cantaloups		●	●	●	●	●	●	●	●	●	●	
Cherries				●	●	●	●	●				
Cranberries	●								●	●	●	●
Grapefruit	●	●	●	●	●	●	●	●	●	●	●	●
Grapes	●	●	●	●	●	●	●	●	●	●	●	●
Honeydews		●	●	●	●	●	●	●	●	●	●	●
Lemons	●	●	●	●	●	●	●	●	●	●	●	●
Limes	●	●	●	●	●	●	●	●	●	●	●	●
Mangoes			●	●	●	●	●	●				
Nectarines	●	●				●	●	●	●	●		
Oranges	●	●	●	●	●	●	●	●	●	●	●	●
Papayas	●	●	●	●	●	●	●	●	●	●	●	●
Peaches					●	●	●	●	●	●		
Pears	●	●	●	●	●	●	●	●	●	●	●	●
Pineapple	●	●	●	●	●	●	●	●	●	●	●	●
Plums						●	●	●	●	●		
Strawberries	●	●	●	●	●	●	●	●	●	●	●	●
Tangerines	●	●	●	●	●	●				●	●	●
Watermelons	●	●	●	●	●	●	●	●	●	●	●	●

ends and underarm seams. These construction details apply to men's and children's clothes as well as women's. Be doubly careful about reinforcements in children's clothes, though. For better wear, you'll want double stitching, taped seams, or bartacking on pocket corners of trousers, in the shoulder seams of T-shirts, at the end of plackets, and in the underarms of shirts and dresses.

One of the main points to remember is that no garment is better than the material it is made of. A garment made of inferior fabric will sag, run, rumple, or tear—and no amount of care will save it. Good material doesn't stretch out of shape, fray, run, or tear apart at the seams under strain. The superior fabrics are the ones whose colors are woven in, rather than stamped on, and whose weave is fine and tight. Watch this last point particularly. Many fabrics are now being chemically treated to give them the appearance of having more body and substance than they actually do. Once these chemicals are washed or cleaned out, you are left with a flimsy, easily crumpled garment.

If you don't trust your eye for judging quality of fabric and workmanship, give yourself a few hours in the most expensive store in town. Try dresses on. Examine them. Have a little fun. Your firsthand look at top quality garments will increase your ability to avoid bad buys.

To profit from sales, to spot bargains, and to know whether something advertised is a real value, you must learn to read every word of an ad. It also helps to know a bit about advertising lingo. A headline may send you chasing after a leather handbag at a fantastically low price, but had you read the entire ad, you'd have realized that your chase was leading to an *imitation* leather handbag. That headline probably said "Genuine Leather Look", or some such ambiguous and misleading term.

Kinds of Sales

There are several kinds of sales, and their names often give you a clue to what you might find in them. Here are a few examples.

Clothes buying can be a pleasure or a frustrating annoyance: by planning your wardrobe needs ahead of time at home and making your shopping trips to take advantage of seasonal sales—or when you have the time and feel inclined to do careful comparison shopping—you can spare yourself those frantic, expensive Saturday afternoons in and out of stores to find something especially for that Saturday night.

39

Seasonal sales offer merchandise that remains after a season has ended. Remember, though, it's to your advantage that the merchandising season does not coincide with the weather outside. So if you get a suit in the famous after-Christmas sale, you still have a few winter months to wear it in, or, if you get a swimsuit in the July sales, you still have some summer months to use it in.

Private sales are for regular or charge customers, and allow them to get merchandise at a sale price before it is offered in a sale to the public. Some department and specialty stores precede almost every general sale with a private one.

Special purchase, *store manager's*, *buyer's*, or *manufacturer's closeout* sales are all much the same thing. As the names indicate, the store has been able to pick up merchandise directly from a manufacturer, without going through a wholesaler, and is passing its savings on to you. You can sometimes find real values in such sales, but be careful. The manufacturer may be overstocked on goods that have not sold well, and may pass off his second-rate merchandise to the retailer, who passes it on to you.

Anniversary sales, as the name suggests, mark a store's founding. *Closeout* sales are designed to clear shelves and racks of last year's models and styles. Closeouts differ from seasonal sales in that what is offered is not necessarily out of season.

Advertising terms can be misleading, and you'll do well to know how to read between the lines. One often-used term in giving a comparative price is "value". You'll see a housecoat offered at $11.95, for example, with the claim that it is a "$17 value". The ad wants to give you the idea that $17 is the usual price of the housecoat, though this may not be the case at all. Even so, the garment may well be worth $11.95; but don't be fooled into thinking it's a big bargain.

Merchandise marked "irregular" or "imperfect" is not to be scorned. Sometimes the flaws in these less-than-perfect goods in no way diminish their appearance or utility. Make a careful examination, of course. A

How many women have bought a dress which looked absolutely perfect until after the first washing or cleaning, and then discovered to their sorrow that the shoddy workmanship showed all over, or that the cheap fabric had lost its original feel and now hung limp and lifeless. The flimsy dress may have a lower price tag, but if you figure out the cost-per-wearing, it frequently turns out to be a very expensive luxury. Using these tips, you can teach yourself to recognize, and avoid paying for, poor workmanship.

slightly flawed pair of tights can be worn under slacks with no one the wiser—except you, as a good shopper. On the other hand, a silk blouse with a pulled thread along the bustline isn't worth it however large the price reduction may be.

Thrift Shops with a Difference

Most large cities have a special kind of women's secondhand clothing shop that makes the word secondhand take on a glow of glamour. These shops carry expensive clothes—often exclusive couturier models from world-famous designers—at great reductions. The clothes are usually hardly worn and in excellent condition—they are discards only because the owners are the types that can't be seen in the same dress twice.

Another kind of thrift shop to explore, if your city is big enough, is one that has clothes with the labels cut out of them. This is usually a sign that the clothing is prestige merchandise that didn't sell well in the better shops. If the offers are genuine—and you do have to trust your eyes to avoid any clinkers—you can save from 25 to 40 per cent of the original price. There are shops like this for men's as well as women's clothes.

As prices keep going up and up it's more important than ever to get the shopping habits that help you economize on everyday food and clothing expenses. You can see from the hints in this chapter that it's still possible to save money without being outright miserly. Perhaps it does take some of the fun out of shopping—but, on the other hand, there's no fun at all in drastic cuts as the alternative to careful buying.

1. Make sure the garment you're buying has generous seam allowance and hem.

2. All raw edges of the fabric should be finished to prevent raveling.

3. Watch that all plaids and stripes are matched precisely at the seams.

4. If the neckline gapes or the shoulders droop —don't buy! These are signs that the garment is too big across the shoulders or upper chest above the bust-line—an area that can't be corrected without enlarging an armhole that is already too large.

5. Make certain there is underlining throughout to hold the garment's shape and prevent seams and darts from pulling the fabric.

6. Look for collars and lapels that stand up, roll, or lie exactly right because they have their own built-in shape.

7. The interfacings should be crisp and sturdy, so that they spring back into shape after you crumple the garment in your hand.

8. Look for a collar constructed in such a way that the top turns slightly over the under-collar all around the seam edges, hiding the under-collar from view.

9. Look for quality zippers and buttons; closely woven seam tapes or lace bindings.

10. Don't buy if the hemline of a sharply pleated skirt is too short. If you ever let the hem down you will probably never get rid of the original creases.

11. A good point to look for is a separate lining attached to the inside of the garment in various places to cover raw edges and provide a finished interior.

12. Avoid a dress that is too short-waisted when there isn't enough seam allowance at the waistline to lower it.

13. Another danger signal—darts or seams that you need to let out but which have been punctured or dipped at the stitching line.

14. Don't buy a garment of synthetic or synthetic blend fabric (with the exception of synthetic knits) that needs to be let out at seams or hem. Original creases can't always be pressed out of such fabrics.

Clothes Buying Tips

To get the most out of your clothing dollar, buy carefully with an eye to quality: these tips will help you choose. And when you bring your purchases home, be sure to store them carefully and wash or have them cleaned as necessary. Proper maintenance is just as important as your mother said to keep your clothes looking good.

LINGERIE

▶ Proportioned slips cost no more, but fit better.
▶ Lingerie made of synthetics washes easily (usually can be machine-washed) dries quickly.
▶ Wool robes must be dry cleaned and need moth protection, so adding to their cost.
▶ Mail order houses often have excellent buys on lingerie, especially panties.

FUR

▶ Good-wearing medium-priced furs include muskrat, badger, nutria, and otter.
▶ Mouton is not only the lowest priced, but also one of the warmest and longest lasting.
▶ Good quality fur should be lustrous, with uniform color to the skin.
▶ Don't buy fur that has matted or scarred areas.
▶ In a quality fur coat, you should hardly notice where the pelts are joined.
▶ Short-haired furs are more expensive, less warm.

SHOES

▶ Calfskin is the best wearing of the popular priced leathers.
▶ Don't buy shoes with paper insoles; a good insole makes a shoe last longer by holding its shape better.
▶ Get a leather lining in the heel.
▶ When shoes get wet, stuff them with paper before setting aside to dry, away from heat; rub leather with oil while drying to keep it soft.
▶ Women's thin-soled shoes will last longer if half-soles are put on before the first wearing.

SYNTHETIC FABRICS

▶ Most synthetics are colorfast, wrinkle resistant, and do not shrink.

▶ Wash-and-wear fabrics can be machine-washed, and usually need no ironing.

▶ Drip-dry fabrics have to be taken out of the washing machine while still wet, and hung dripping; the water running off helps smooth out wrinkles in the fabric.

▶ Permanent press synthetics save cleaning bills, for even slacks and jackets can be done at home; don't pay the extra initial cost for permanent press finish however, if you always send shirts out to be done.

▶ Polyester and cotton is generally the best quality. blend for fully satisfactory wash-and-wear

▶ Be careful of using chlorine bleaches on synthetics; if the label says to avoid chlorine, use no bleach or a non-chlorine one.

SHIRTS

▶ Pockets should be reinforced at the edge.

▶ Stitches should be short and straight, and button holes evenly and closely stitched.

▶ Solid colors are generally the best value in price and washability.

▶ Wash-and-wears of treated cotton don't usually wear as well as drip-dry polyester and cotton, which also usually looks neater.

▶ If cuffs fray, either turn them or cut the sleeves to short length.

SOCKS

▶ Synthetics wear well, but are not as absorbent as cotton; ban-lon is the most absorbent of the man-made fibers.

▶ Lisle cotton wears longest, and is smoother than plain cotton.

▶ Be sure the foot is knit closely, and the top ribbed closely.

▶ *Spandex* elastic tops wear better.

▶ Turn socks inside out to make sure they are well finished, with toes and heels that are reinforced or double woven.

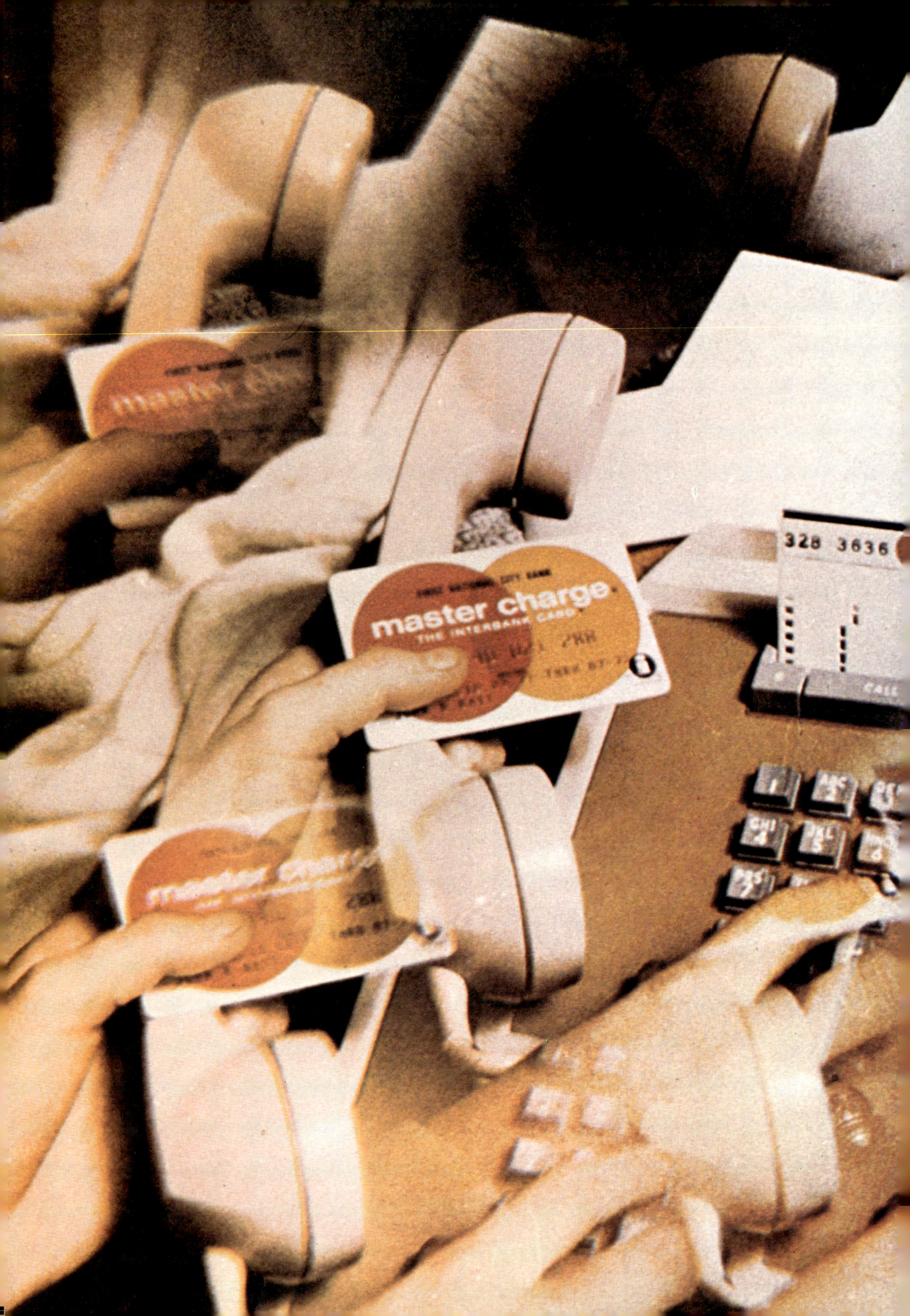
master charge
THE INTERBANK CARD
328 3636

Credit Buying
3

Credit is part and parcel of today's way of life. The use of credit cards, like the one pictured, is now a commonplace. This often leads to increased spending, so it's vital to learn how to handle credit wisely if you are to manage your money well.

Credit was not invented by us Americans. (The ancient Sumerians were into it some 5500 years ago.) Moreover, Mr. & Mrs. Average American of only 50 years ago neither wanted, nor would be able to get, much in the way of credit. Yet, today, credit is the lubricant for the wheels of industry—and the stuff of which the reality of the American dream is made.

In many minds, credit is thought of purely as installment buying. However, credit comes in many different forms. It can be a cash loan, a charge account, a credit card, or deferred payment for services, such as dental treatment. One kind of credit might cost you less than another kind, but all credit costs something. You can make a savings by shopping around for the cheapest credit—but you'll save the most by using credit wisely. This means that you should not borrow money except for emergencies, and that you should buy for cash whenever you can. Limit your installment buying, and stagger major purchases so that you aren't trying to pay for a car, a freezer, a stereo set, and a bedroom suite all at once. When you must use credit, shop for the best buy.

One of the first things you will discover when you begin shopping for credit is that lenders want a solid citizen—someone who stays in one place, holds a steady job, and shows no inclination to skip town with the cash. A secretary, even if she has only been working a short time, usually has an easier time getting a loan than an entertainer. Even if they have been at it for years, entertainers are generally considered bad credit risks because they often have long periods of unemployment, whether or not they make a

IS YOUR RECORDER DAMAGING YOUR CASSETTES?
THE NEW CASSETTE TAPE GUARDIAN PROTECTS YOUR
AMPEX
Scotch Hi-Fi Tape
SONY
TRIO

lot when they do work. Anyone who owns a house finds it easier to get credit than someone who rents. Anyone living in a furnished room is suspect in the eyes of lenders, who assume the prospective borrower has never been able to get together the cash to establish a real home. A credit record, like your general reputation, follows you throughout life. You have to work to keep your record good, but, if you want the things credit can bring, it's worth the effort.

How Much Debt Can You Handle?
Economics experts say that a person can usually manage debts up to 20 per cent of

Left: hi-fi equipment is high on the list of wanted things in a modern home—and it seems like this young couple is about to decide on a set. It's almost certain they'll buy it on the installment plan.

Below: it is the young family with more needs than money that leans most heavily on credit buying, as this chart shows. Typically, the use of credit falls off as household heads near their retirement age.

take-home pay less any mortgage payments. This applies to you only if you can be reasonably sure that your income won't take a nosedive, if you have adequate health insurance, and if you have a nest egg for emergencies. These "ifs" are important, and, because no one can be sure what the future holds, it is safer to keep your debt load between nothing and 15 per cent.

Know How Much Interest You Will Have to Pay Out
Different lenders have different ways of applying interest charges, and as you shop for credit, you may find yourself confused by annual percentage rates, unpaid balances, and true costs. You'll wish you had paid more attention in high school math class, but it's not too late to learn.

One general principle to keep in mind is that monthly interest rates are often quoted at $1\frac{1}{2}$ to $2\frac{1}{2}$ per cent per month. Sounds cheap. Is it? Those percentages are only for one

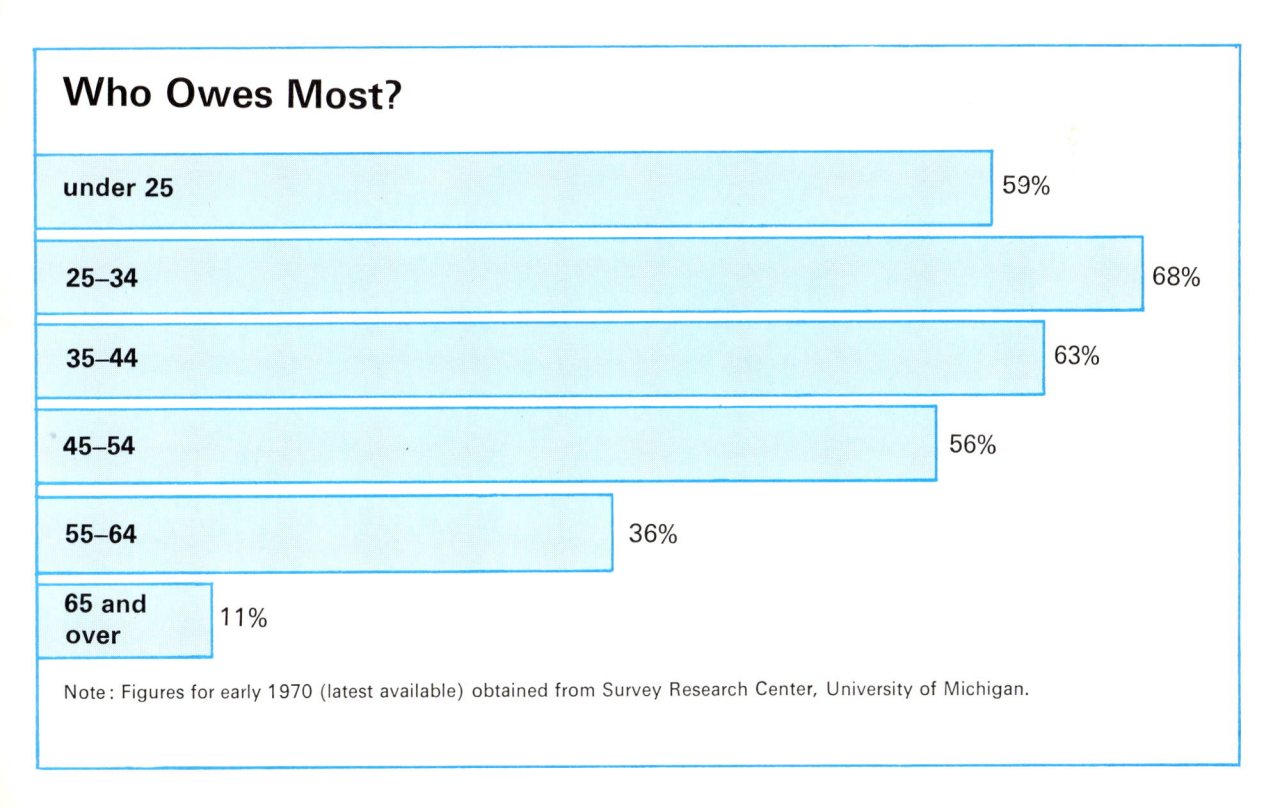

Who Owes Most?

Age	Percentage
under 25	59%
25–34	68%
35–44	63%
45–54	56%
55–64	36%
65 and over	11%

Note: Figures for early 1970 (latest available) obtained from Survey Research Center, University of Michigan.

The Main Credit Buys

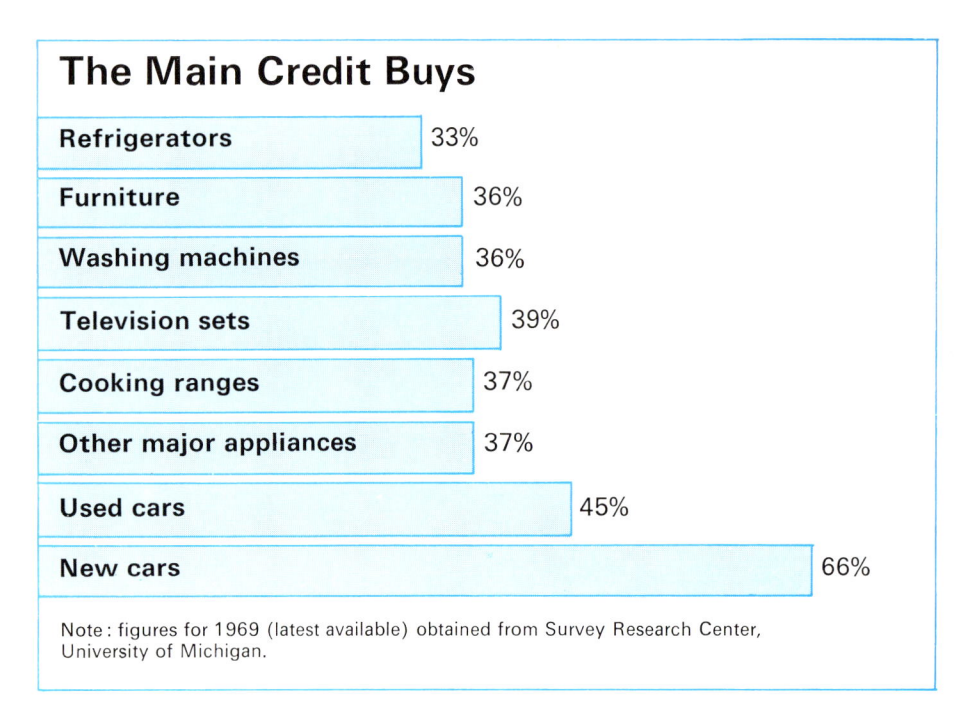

Refrigerators	33%
Furniture	36%
Washing machines	36%
Television sets	39%
Cooking ranges	37%
Other major appliances	37%
Used cars	45%
New cars	66%

Note: figures for 1969 (latest available) obtained from Survey Research Center, University of Michigan.

Left: about a third of all major appliances are purchased on credit, and well over half of all the new cars that are sold.

Right: each time that a credit transaction is completed, a contract along the lines of the one printed here is filled out. Before you sign such a contract, make sure that you clearly understand exactly what you are agreeing to. That means reading all the fine print thoroughly. Credit forms vary from company to company, and from state to state, but all of them will be similar to this sample one.

month. To find the true cost, multiply by 12. The cost at $1\frac{1}{2}$ per cent per month is the same as 18 per cent per year true interest. At $2\frac{1}{2}$ per cent per month, the true annual interest is 30 per cent. Monthly rates of $1\frac{1}{2}$ per cent are often charged when you pay *interest on the unpaid balance*, as for many department store charge accounts, credit cards, and installment plans.

Now for a few other examples of how interest costs work out.

Nancy Hill wanted to take an advanced ballroom dancing course costing $200. She borrowed this amount from the local bank, which charged *simple interest* of 6 per cent. On this basis, the total interest came to $12, and the total loan to $212. Nancy had to pay the full $212 in one sum at the end of the year, but she was happy to work the loan this way because the true interest charge remained at 6 per cent. This method of borrowing, while one of the cheapest, is not readily available to any except those who have an excellent credit rating, and, usually, a long-standing relationship with the bank.

When Edith Mansfield urged her husband to borrow $200 to take advantage of a special one-time offer on the fiberglass canoe he had long dreamed of, she learned what *interest in advance*, or *discounted interest*, meant. The lender quoted a 6 per cent interest charge, and immediately took that amount—$12— off the $200. The Mansfields had use of only $188, but their twelve monthly installments of $16.66 each (one-twelfth of $200) meant that they were paying interest on the full amount. The true interest rate came to 11.78 per cent.

Still another method of calculating interest was presented to Joan Fisher. With her husband's approval, she decided to borrow $200 to pay for an unusual summer science course for their teenage daughter. She was required to pay by *add-on interest* at 6 per cent. In this case, the twelve monthly payments were $17.66 each. ($16.66 is one-twelfth of $200, the capital, and $1 is one-twelfth of $12, the interest). Joan was paying interest on the total amount of the loan each month, even though she had reduced the balance each month. The true interest rate, then, was 11.08 per cent.

Let's tackle the whole question of interest charges from another angle, by shopping together for a dishwasher that costs $300. You decide to pay $50 down, and borrow $250. You ask the appliance dealer what he would charge over a two-year period, and

Seller's Name: _____
_____

Contract* _____

Retail Installment Contract and Security Agreement

The undersigned (herein called Purchaser, whether one or more) purchases from _____
_____ (seller)
and grants to _____
a security interest in, subject to the terms and conditions hereof, the following described property.

QUANTITY	DESCRIPTION	AMOUNT
Description of Trade-in:		
	Sales Tax	
	Total	

Insurance Agreement

The purchase of insurance coverage is voluntary and not required for credit. (Type of Ins), insurance coverage is available at a cost of $ _____ for the term of credit.

☐ I desire insurance coverage
Signed _____ Date _____

☐ I do not desire insurance coverage
Signed _____ Date _____

Notice to Buyer: You are entitled to a copy of the contract you sign. You have the right to pay in advance the unpaid balance of this contract and obtain a partial refund of the finance charge based on the "Actuarial Method."
[Any other method of computation may be so identified, for example, "Rule of 78's", "Sum of the Digits", etc.]

PURCHASER'S NAME _____
PURCHASER'S ADDRESS _____
CITY _____ STATE _____ ZIP _____

1. CASH PRICE $ _____
2. LESS: CASH DOWN PAYMENT $ _____
3. TRADE-IN _____
4. TOTAL DOWN PAYMENT $ _____
5. UNPAID BALANCE OF CASH PRICE $ _____
6. OTHER CHARGES:
   _____
   _____ $ _____
7. AMOUNT FINANCED $ _____
8. FINANCE CHARGE $ _____
9. TOTAL OF PAYMENTS $ _____
10. DEFERRED PAYMENT PRICE (1+6+8) $ _____
11. ANNUAL PERCENTAGE RATE _____ %

Purchaser hereby agrees to pay to _____
_____ at their offices shown above the 'TOTAL OF PAYMENTS" shown above in _____ monthly installments of $ _____ (final payment to be $ _____) the first installment being payable _____ 19_____ and all subsequent installments on the same day of each consecutive month until paid in full. The finance charge applies from _____ (Date)

Signed _____

you find that his true annual interest rate is 18.3 per cent. This means you will owe $45 in credit costs.

Next, you go to your bank and ask what you will be charged for a $250 personal loan for two years. The answer is 12.59 per cent, or $38.56. (This includes a small charge for credit insurance.) You then try your credit union, and find out you can get the $250 for a charge of 12 per cent. Over the two-year period this will cost $32.45. Finally, remembering the ad you saw for a finance company, you ask about its promised "low" monthly interest charges. You discover that 24.6 per cent is their true annual interest rate, which means your $250 loan would cost $79.22 over a two-year period. You borrow from the credit union in the happy realization that, if you had not shopped so carefully, you could have overspent by $46.77. This shows the difference between expensive credit, and relatively low-cost credit.

The Credit Contract
Contract language can scare anyone, but self-protection demands that you give understanding it a good try. A recent federal law is on your side to get past some of the tricks of credit contracts: the Truth in Lending Act. The most important provision of this law is that lenders must give borrowers credit costs, called the "financial charge", in dollars. They must also state the charges as an "annual percentage rate". This not only shows you the exact dollars-and-cents cost to you, but the percentage figure also helps you make comparisons with credit rates of other dealers, stores, and banks.

It may be "elementary, my dear Watson", but it's worth a warning that there should be no blanks left in the contract for the lender to fill in later. Look for these items in black-and-white: the purchase price or the amount borrowed; interest or service charges in dollars and per cent; down payment; trade-in allowance; insurance charges, if any; any other costs or service charges; total amount due; amount of each payment; and the date each payment is due. Any lender who skips

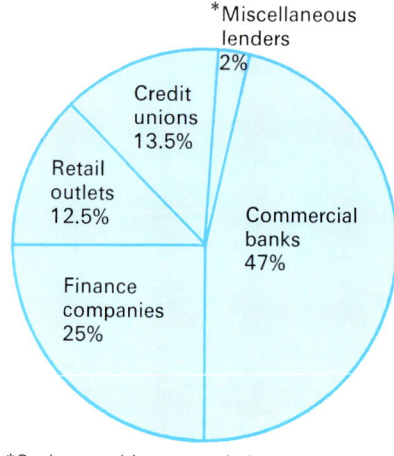

*Savings and loan associations and mutual savings banks.

Data: Federal Reserve System, 1972

Above: these government figures show how much Americans owed at the end of 1972 on loans taken out for installment buying. At the same time, the chart shows that commercial banks are the favorite source for credit loans.

Right: pawnshops are known for paying far below value on things pawned. Their main attraction as a source of loans is the speed with which they give ready cash.

information on a contract is in violation of the law.

Where Can You Get Hard Cash?
When the kind of credit you want is hard cash, you have a number of sources to shop, though there are some limitations on all of them. One source you may not have thought of is your insurance—though a loan is given only on cash value policies. (See Chapter 6.)

Banks will give personal loans to both depositors and nondepositors, but only when the borrower is considered a good credit risk. In the case of a "pass book" loan from a bank, you borrow against your own savings, and your savings account is the collateral, or security, that the bank will keep if you don't repay. The advantage of a pass book loan is that your account continues to draw interest, even though the money in it is blocked for the period of the loan. On a regular loan from a bank, you can pledge such property as your life insurance, US Savings Bonds, other bonds, stocks, or mutual fund shares as collateral. If you have no collateral, or have used it to get another loan, the bank will generally ask for a co-signer, who is just as responsible as you are for seeing that the loan is repaid, and legally must do so if you default on your payment.

Personal finance and small loan companies take much greater credit risks than banks. They also require less collateral, but charge substantially higher interest rates and service charges. Credit unions are noted for low interest rates, but borrowers must be members, and membership is restricted—usually to a single firm or organization.

On the bottom of the list of where to look for ready cash are pawnshops. They charge high rates, and lend a much smaller amount than any collateral is worth.

The Credit Card Craze
There are 300 million credit cards in use in America today. With two or three different ones, you can buy or pay for just about anything—traffic tickets in Phoenix, real estate taxes in Pima County, Arizona, sandwiches in Yosemite National Park, airline tickets, dinners, dancing, groceries,

health care, and on and on. The temptations assailing the holder of a credit card are innumerable, and it has been found that credit card users spend 30 per cent more than cash customers. Yet, the attraction of the little plastic cards seems irresistible. In fact, paper money seems to be getting the shove.

Because of the convenience of credit cards, we don't always stop to think of cost—both in charges for credit and in the increase of spending. It's easy to play down cost, too, since just about all credit card systems charge nothing extra if you pay the full bill when it is due. If you don't though, you pay steep interest rates, commonly as high as 18 per cent annually. In addition, you have to pay a given annual fee for certain cards.

There are three basic types of credit cards: the bank card, the travel and entertainment card (T&E), and the one-purpose card. Bank cards are easy to come by, and are free if you pay the bills on time. You can use them in retail stores, restaurants, beauty shops, and any other place sporting a decal of the card you carry.

The T&E card—such as Diners Club or American Express—is neither as easy to get, or keep, as the bank card. In the first place, you must apply for one. Secondly, you must measure up to income and credit ratings. Thirdly, you must pay a yearly fee of up to $20. For all their cost, T&E cards are the love of businessmen and frequent travelers. To pay for a client's lunch in Albuquerque on a flying trip from Philadelphia, or to stay at a better hotel in St. Louis after two dismal visits, seem to be reason enough.

The one-purpose card is issued by a single

company, perhaps an oil firm, a department store, or a car rental agency. You can only buy or use the products of the issuing organization. Of course, in the case of oil companies, you can use the card anywhere in the country. You pay nothing for the one-purpose card, but usually your credit must be good to get one.

Before protective federal legislation was passed in 1970, many people found themselves the victims of credit card abuse. What usually happened was that their credit cards were stolen, and the thieves bought as much as they could before the card number appeared on a "hot card sheet". At that point, further credit was stopped—and the innocent credit card holder was automatically put down as a bad credit risk!

The 1970 law limits your liability as a credit card holder to $50 if your card has been misued by someone else. Furthermore, if you notify the organization that issued the card of its loss or theft *before* someone starts to use it for thievery, you are not liable at all. You protect yourself most against possible credit card abuse by reporting at once the loss or theft of any of your credit cards.

In addition, the law prohibits the issuance of credit cards except "in response to a request or application". If some unscrupulous outfit still sends you an unwanted credit card through the mails, you can now toss it away without fear that a thief will dig it out of the garbage and use it. In this case, you are doubly covered: the issuer is in the wrong for sending you an unsolicited card, and your credit rating is safe in case someone runs a bill up by using that unsolicited card.

Left: among the great conveniences of credit cards is the international service that many offer. This man is buying his gas at a South American station with his United States credit card.

Right: although federal laws protect you against misuse of your credit cards, it is only good sense to destroy an old card when a new one is issued. Cutting it clear through guarantees that no one else can use it.

The Big Buy
4

Americans enjoy a high standard of living envied by most of the rest of the world. Ask yourself what this good life is made up of, and you're sure to list owning a home and a car, eating and dressing well, having good furniture and furnishings, and enjoying the comfort and convenience of modern equipment including refrigerators and freezers, washing machines, dishwashers, and air conditioning.

As the price swing continues upward, the good life seems harder to reach, and to hold on to. The big buys—a house (see Chapter 5), furniture, carpeting, major household appliances, and a car—either keep getting more expensive, or cost more and more to service, or both. In fact, consumer expert Sidney Margolius says in his book *The Consumer's Guide to Better Buying*: "When you come down to it . . . the actual shopping dilemmas of consumers in the 1970's are worse than ever in the thirty-five years I have reported on these problems."

Is it hopeless, then? No, just harder. The tips in this chapter are about the large purchases you make. You'll find that smart shopping is mostly a matter of making the thoughtful instead of the hasty buy, of comparing values, and of knowing how to look for and recognize good quality.

Do Some Research

You want good value, whatever you spend, so the question generally becomes: can you find the product that fills your needs and suits your pocketbook, too? One of the ways of going about making a sound buying decision is to do some research on your own.

It's not as hard or dry as it sounds. There

Buying a car can be an exciting project, but make sure that talking airily about thousands of dollars doesn't take your mind off the savings you can make in tens, by shrewd bargaining and sensible selection of optional accessories.

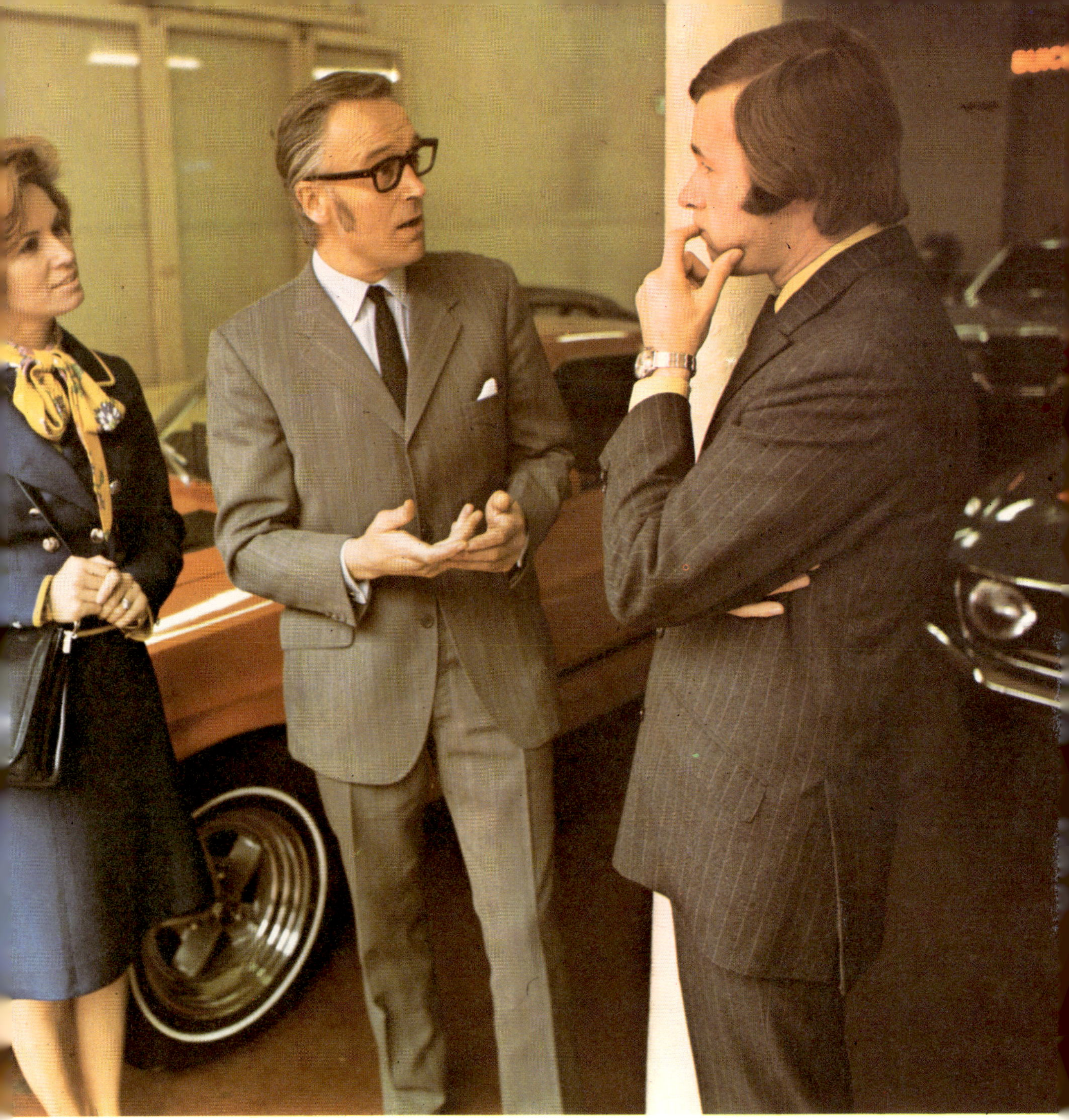

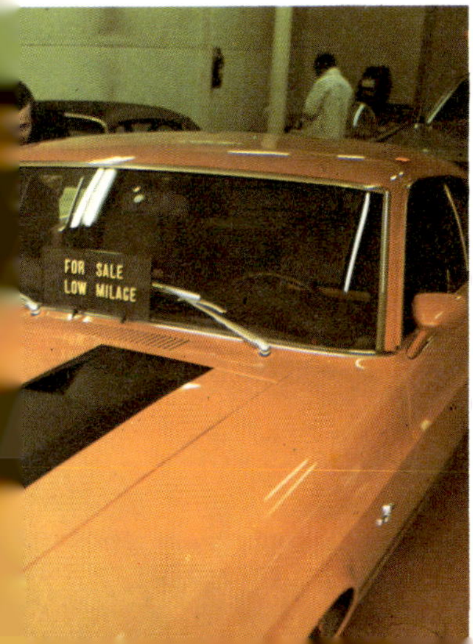
FOR SALE
LOW MILAGE

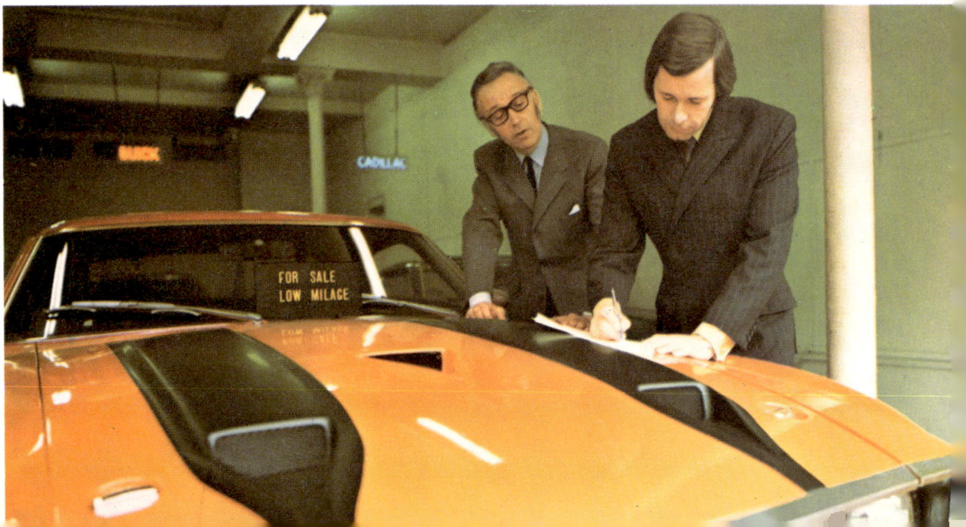
BUICK
CADILLAC
FOR SALE
LOW MILAGE

are a number of publications that can help you make better buying decisions, and they are often available at your local library. You can even buy them if you prefer. (See the reading list at the end of this book for some titles of useful buying guides.)

Perhaps the handiest and easiest start for you is to refer to the monthly magazine, *Consumer Reports*, which also puts out an annual summary called *Consumer Reports Buying Guide*. In its monthly issues, this publication reviews six or seven items, comparing different brands in each category, as well as different models of the same brand. It describes available products thoroughly, and explains the differences between them. In doing so, the magazine emphasizes which differences are important, and why. All this is done in clear language, even when dealing with technical matters. Because *Consumer Reports* repeats studies periodically, especially on big-expense items, you can usually get information on current models.

Consumer Reports is also useful if you decide to buy something secondhand. Just look in the back issues and last year's *Buying Guide* for the item you want, and find the models that were rated most reliable when new. Of course, there is no guarantee that even highly rated models will not have been misused by former owners; but, on the other hand, a model that was not first-rate when new could hardly prove satisfactory the second time around.

Guarantees and Warranties: What They Mean

Say you have decided which make to buy, and have compared values at more than one department store or dealer. You are on the verge of closing the sale. Before you do, thoroughly and thoughtfully read any guarantee and/or warranty you get.

Warranties are usually issued by a manufacturer, and state the extent of his liability for the product. Sometimes this warranty is all you get, usually in the form of a card that has to be mailed back to the manufacturer. Sometimes, however, the seller, assembler, or distributor of merchandise issues a guarantee. This guarantee very likely will include the manufacturer's warranty, and may or may not have further protection offered by the issuing agent.

Before you buy, you should know what is covered, how long your protection lasts, and whether it is the maker or seller who will make repairs or replace guaranteed parts. Read every word carefully. Sometimes the fact that the guarantee is for parts only is in such fine print that you might overlook it. That can be your undoing, because many labor charges for installing the guaranteed parts are outrageously high.

Reading the fine print and understanding the guarantee can't save you if you are careless. Helen Martin is a case in point, although luck took a hand to bring about a happy ending for her. Helen bought an expensive color television, but did not bother to mail the warranty card back to the manufacturer. Neither did she keep the sales slip from the local dealer. Eleven months later, the picture tube blew—and so did Helen. She phoned the dealer and raged about the shoddy product, but could not give him the date of purchase so that he could check his records. Nonetheless, he managed to discover the date, and informed her that the tube would be replaced free, just as guaranteed, because the warranty was for one year. Helen was elated, of course, and realized that she had a gem of an honest dealer who did more than she had any right to expect in the situation. Don't count on being this lucky. Mail all guarantee or warranty cards directly after you make a purchase. Also, keep a file of sales slips and

---

A preliminary visit around the stores, taking a look at what's available and picking up all the leaflets, makes comparison shopping much easier. You can sit at home in comfort with your shoes off and a cup of coffee and figure out exactly which models do what you want, so that your next visit to the store can be a straightforward inspection of the models that you are interested in, and ready to buy.

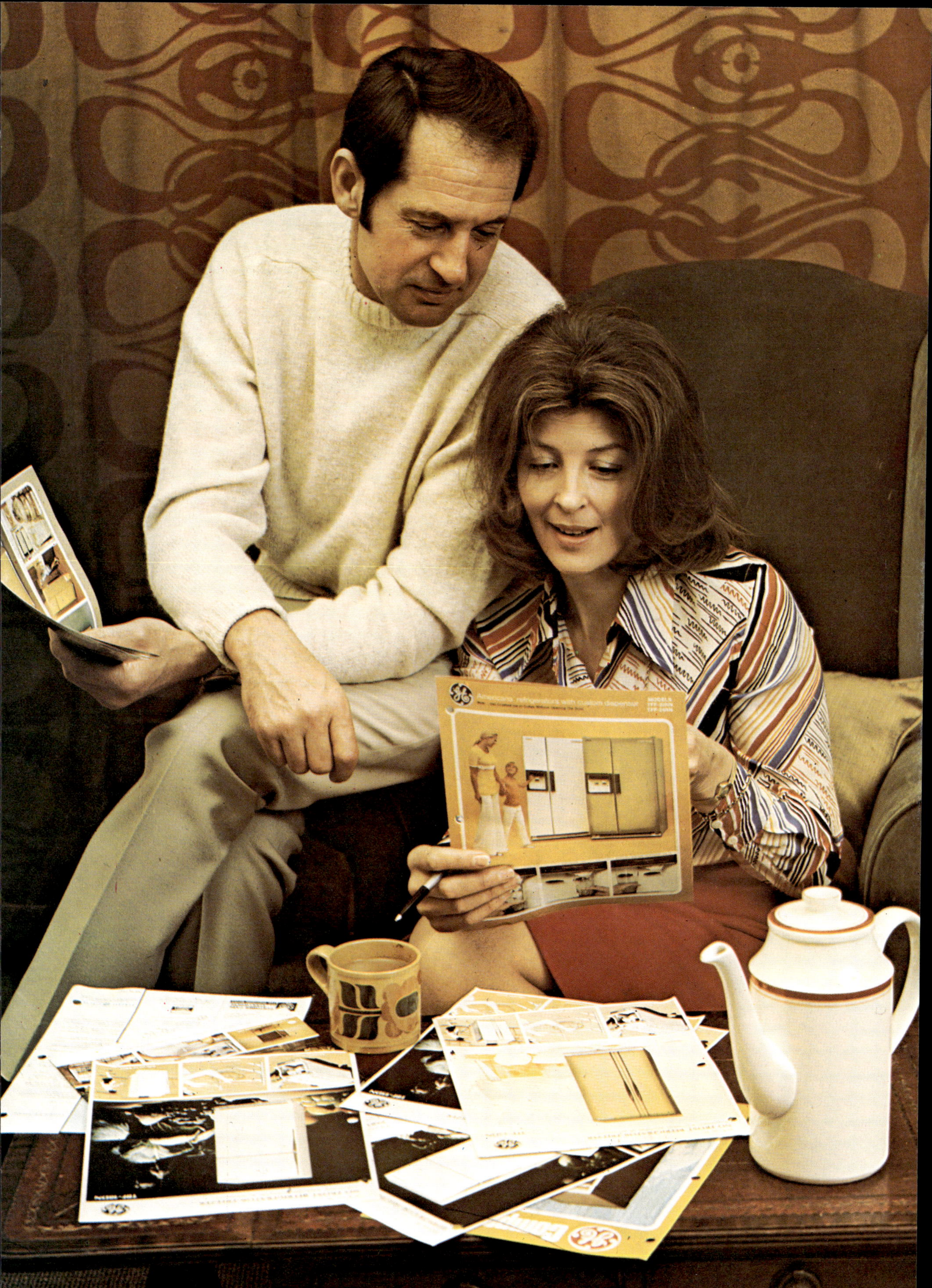

canceled checks for all major purchases so that you can prove when and where you bought them, and what you paid.

Furniture: Interior Beauty at What Cost?

Your home is where you spend most of your free time, pursue your personal interests, raise your family, and entertain your friends. It reflects your taste and your way of life. To achieve the beauty and comfort you want, you will make a substantial outlay for furniture and furnishings.

Every bit of expert advice ever given says to buy quality furniture. That means good material and sound construction over faddishness in design and color. It usually means higher price, but although you pay more, you will get longer and more satisfying service. Even for young couples starting out, the experts advise investment in quality. Getting pieces slowly—even one at a time—may seem a bit dreary and self-sacrificing, but the ultimate pleasures are the greater.

Another thing to consider, especially for the first-time home furnishers, is that tastes are bound to change from time to time. If your basic pieces are well-built, and have simple, clean lines, you can accommodate your taste changes by varying the accessories. You can also go along with the latest way-out fashion in color, fabric, and design of accessories if the main big pieces have the timelessness of good taste and quality.

Would you like to buy a $750 sofa made by a nationally known manufacturer for about 40 per cent off? You can do it if you mark time, keep an eye open for the ads, and then act quickly when you spot a *warehouse sale* of a leading furniture or department store. Keep in mind that the warehouse may be distant and hard to find. But, once there, you can often get furniture of a better quality than you could normally afford.

Don't expect a wide choice of style, fabric, color, and wood at a warehouse sale. The pieces offered are often one-of-a-kind, so you will have to settle strictly for what's there. Of course, if savings on a chair or sofa are great

Take a good look at furniture before you buy: check that it is constructed solidly, that the fabric is of good quality, and that the size is right for where you'll put it.

enough, you can consider reupholstering or slipcovering to get the fabric and color you want. There might also be some nicks or dents in the wood, but generally the condition of furniture in warehouse sales is good.

To reupholster the furniture you bought in such a sale, your best bet is to watch for *custom upholstery sales.* Many department stores run upholstery sales or specials about twice a year. The purpose of these sales is to make room for new fabrics, patterns, and colors. The range of materials on sale may be slightly limited, but you will save from 15 to 30 per cent on what you do find.

More and more smart buyers are turning to secondhand furniture and household equipment as the way to keep costs down.

They have found that secondhand is far from second best. For example, imagine an elderly childless couple who have had an elegant home for many years. They decide to move into a small apartment, and put an ad in the paper to get rid of the bulk of their household treasures. This could be a treasure trove for you, because you are likely to get high quality at bargain prices.

In our generally mobile society, people frequently sell off all their furnishings, rather than move them from place to place. If you watch the newspaper classified ads, you can often find excellent used furniture from diplomats, armed services personnel, or others on the move. The main drawback is that you must arrange for pickup and delivery yourself. Also you get no guarantees, which can be risky with appliances, but careful inspection can go a long way toward reducing risk—and the savings are usually enough to make taking a chance worth it.

Right: buying unfinished furniture and painting or staining it exactly as you want it is not only an economical way to furnish a house, but offers a lot of creative satisfaction to the ones who do it.

Below: country auctions can be a fine place to acquire unusual pieces at cheaper prices than you would find in the city—but be sure you make up your mind about what any piece is worth to you before the excitement of bidding gets underway, and then stick strictly to the limit you have set for yourself.

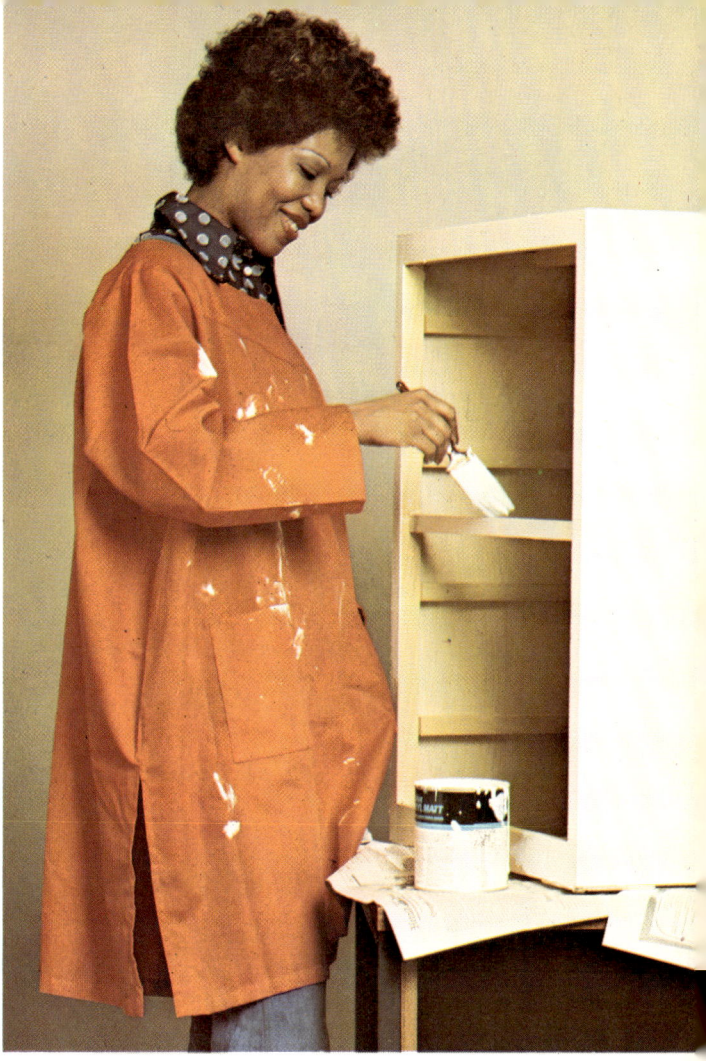

Thrift shops and Salvation Army stores are other possible sources for good used furniture and appliances. Some may even deliver, or arrange for delivery, at a modest additional cost.

There is one golden rule for the specialist in secondhand shopping: go for the best you can find. Products that were cheap and shoddy to begin with only get worse with use. Top quality products can withstand a great deal of wear, and often get a mellowness that adds to their charm. Look for good graining in the wood and veneer—and examine the unexposed part of the wood, too, to make sure there are no hidden defects. Give chairs, benches, and sofas a firm shake to see if legs fit tightly. If the furniture is jointed, get your husband to make sure the joints are of the mortise and tenon type—or, even better, dowelled. Furniture with butt joints—that is, with the two pieces of wood brought flush together and screwed or glued—is not worth the price, new or used.

A good time to make a start in buying secondhand is when you furnish a spare room, change from nursery to children's bedroom, or equip the den with a refrigerator of its own. The young couple just starting out may also want to carefully consider used furnishings. Doing so would enable them to save up to buy better things when their tastes are more set, and their lives more settled.

Another money-saving device is to buy unfinished furniture. Chests of drawers, bookshelves, and desks are often good buys, and it can be fun to finish them in the exact color or wood grain you want. Some of the unfinished furniture today is not only reasonable in price, but also of good design and construction—waiting only for your imagina-

Buying a carpet is a major purchase for any home, and like all major purchases, requires a lot of homework to make a sensible choice. Be sure that you are buying the right quality for the right place: there is no point in buying a carpet designed for light use to put down on the stairs, nor in spending more for top quality to carpet the spare room. Remember you must have the right underlay to get proper wear from the carpet.

tion and skill to transform it into an attractive and useful part of your life.

What's Underfoot?

The biggest home decorating problem and expense, aside from furniture, is usually carpeting. The overriding fashion for wall-to-wall carpeting often puts the home furnisher into a quandry. If a compromise is made on quality, the carpeting will wear poorly. If good quality is the criterion, the cost can go sky high.

The main advantages of rugs are that they are less costly; they can be changed around to distribute wear at heavy traffic spots; they are easier to send out for professional cleaning; and they can be easily transported in a move. In fact, many couples, especially young homemakers, have taken to the current fashion of area rugs, which are smaller than room size.

Whether you decide on wall-to-wall carpeting or rugs, you will have to consider fabric and texture. Nylon—if you make absolutely sure it is continuous-filament nylon—wears just about as well as wool these days. However, wool still has the edge over all other fabrics in soil resistance and lack of pilling. Some of the new acrylic and polyester fabrics are fairly good wearing. Rayon and cotton wear the least well, but they are generally low priced, and are suitable for low-traffic areas in the home.

Texture is simply a matter of personal taste, since it has little to do with the durability of carpeting or rugs. Of course, some loop and novelty textures do prove more difficult to clean, but the way your floor covering looks to you has a lot to do with the satisfaction and pleasure you'll get from it.

A carpet savings tip: most stores dealing in carpets wind up their sales year with hundreds of yards of "short" or "roll" ends, which are the last pieces off the roll from the factory; these are usually large enough to make an area rug. The stores bind these ends on four sides, and sell them once a year at great savings per foot—sometimes up to 50 per cent. It doesn't take much figuring to see

Did you ever stop to think how long your household appliances ought to last? Knowing the life expectancy of such equipment is important to your overall buying plans. The chart figures show you the average age of the most-used home appliances.

how you can use these brand new pieces for wall-to-wall carpeting. It might take some work, and there might also be an extra seam or so. At the end, however, you'll have the wall-to-wall floor covering you want at, perhaps, half the price.

One reputable New York store showed how its customers, buying roll ends, could put down 12 × 21 feet of carpeting that once would have cost $308 at the low cost of $139.

When choosing floor coverings, shop at several stores to compare prices and quality. Remember that carpeting has very little resale value. The exception is Oriental rugs, which can often be sold for more than you paid; but you have to know how to buy them, and you have to pay a great deal in the first place. The best way to preserve carpets and rugs, as well as draperies and upholstery, is by regular cleaning. Nothing wears out fabric faster than dirt.

Major Appliances
A house may be a home, but it can surely be a tough place to live in without the convenience and comfort provided by modern appliances. One important consideration in buying appliances is that, each year, they cost more to repair than the year before, because of rises in servicing charges. The aim, then, is to get home appliances that will be as trouble-free as possible. To do so, careful shopping is necessary. For the wise shopper, it is an absolute must to research brand and model ratings in *Consumer Reports*, as a preliminary to shopping. Then arm yourself with some of the following suggestions on what to look for in good home appliances.

Refrigerators. Measure the space you have available for the refrigerator and decide whether a right- or left-hand door is best. The storage capacity must meet your family needs. A family with two children needs eight cubic feet of fresh food space—but two more cubic feet are handy if entertaining is frequent. Unless you own a separate freezer, the freezer compartment of the refrigerator should allow two cubic feet per family member. Although it is more expensive than the standard refrigerator, a combination refrigerator and freezer is a good buy if you have no food freezer. The following basic features are important to good operation of a refrigerator: seamless exterior construction of porcelain enamel; corrosion-resistant aluminum or plastic shelves; rust-resistant metal or plastic baskets and drawers that are easily removed for cleaning; odorless, moisture-resistant insulation of glass wool, glass fiber, or foam; and sturdy door hinges. Make certain the freezer space is a separate insulated compartment, with a tight-fitting door, and a cooling system that maintains 0°F temperature. Watch for adequate ice cube space. Remember, the more gadgets a refrigerator—or any other appliance—sports, the more expensive it will be. Does the egg rack really have to be in a contrasting color?

Deep Freezers. If you are a family of four or more, a freezer can be a great convenience. It allows you to buy specials in quantity, to cut down on the number of trips you make to the supermarket, and to store seasonal fruits and vegetables in quantity. You can also freeze homemade meals and home-baked goodies. This is a great boon to the working mother, and can come in handy for unexpected company, too.

16

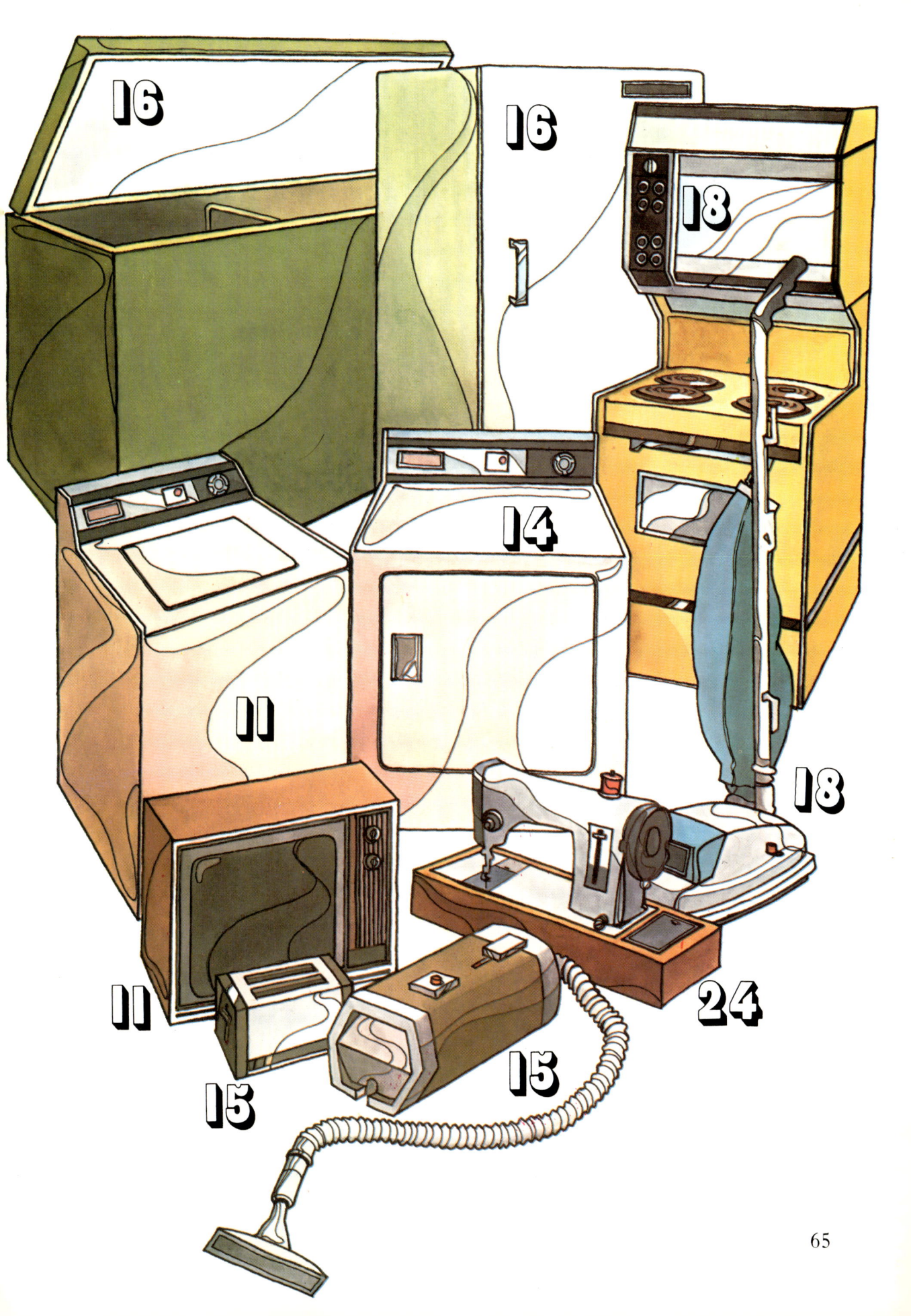

16

18

14

11

11

18

15

15

24

65

Left: if, like many families, you have a small kitchen, it is particularly important that you measure (and measure again!) before you buy any appliances. Plan where you'll fit them in; if there's a door, decide which way is most convenient for opening; and if you're buying a small machine for using on the counter work out where you'll put it when it's not actually being used.

Right: it's easy to be dazzled by the rows of shiny new appliances down at the store. To keep a grip on yourself, before you go shopping write down what your requirements are, and what the maximum dimensions can be to fit.

Before buying a freezer at all, however, be warned that it takes planning and work to get the full value out of it. You have to shop carefully to keep the freezer stocked to at least 80 per cent of capacity, which is good economy, and you must pack foods painstakingly so that you can find them again when you want them. You also have to specially wrap and label what you store. In all, it takes brain, muscle, and time to make the large purchase cost of a freezer worth it. Most city families and small families of less than four should probably forget about a freezer, and buy a big refrigerator with a good-sized built-in freezing unit instead.

The upright freezer is more expensive than the chest type, but easier to defrost if it is not a frost-free type. The chest type takes more floor space, and, because its contents are packed more closely, makes it harder to locate specific items. The chest type is also cheaper to operate since it retains the cold better when opened, and thus uses less electricity keeping the temperature right.

The size of freezer you should buy depends on the size of your family. A rule of thumb is to allow three to four cubic feet of space for each family member if you plan to shop once a week, and five to six cubic feet if you shop less frequently, or plan to freeze home-grown foods. Make certain the floor supporting the freezer can hold 1000 pounds, the average weight of a fully-stocked freezer. The construction features important in refrigerators also apply to freezers.

Beware of freezer plans. They have been heavily promoted as a way of cutting food costs, but they have rarely proved to do so. When you join a food freezer plan, you generally pay a membership fee that is supposed to allow you to buy the freezer, and food, at wholesale cost. However, the files of the Federal Trade Commission, Better Business Bureaus, and State Attorney General's Offices bulge with cases of fraud and misrepresentation. You will probably do better to buy independent of a food plan.

Washing Machines. Automatic washers are the greatest invention ever for saving on laundry bills, and wear and tear on the housewife. The most popular kind is the fully automatic, in which one setting of the controls is all that is needed to fill the tub, wash, rinse, damp-dry, and drain. Washers come with a bewildering choice of controls for different fabrics and temperatures. The more controls on a machine, the more expensive it will be, the greater the possibility of a breakdown, and the more it will cost to repair. To have your washer work better and last longer, plan to wash delicate fabrics by hand, and use commercial machines for heavy rugs, blankets, and other such items. A load of heavy articles can throw a washer badly out of kilter unless it is especially built for heavy duty use.

A washer and dryer combined in one unit is also available. It has been found over the years that many of the washer-dryer combinations have performed unsatisfactorily. The major complaint is that one breakdown stops you from either washing or drying. On the other hand, this type of machine is clearly smaller and cheaper than two separate units. The size might be an important consideration if space is short.

The most important construction feature to check out is the safety mechanism that stops the machine when the door is opened. Whether you choose a top- or front-load type is a matter of pure choice, since both seem to be equally efficient. Regardless of style, a machine should have easily adjustable legs so that it can be properly leveled without a major engineering job; a drain strainer to catch lint and soil; rinse controls, which are important for synthetic fabrics; and a tight seal to prevent water leaks. Never buy any electrical appliance that does not carry the symbol of approval of the Underwriters' Laboratories, Inc. (abbreviated as UL or ULI).

Dishwashers. Dishwashers have long since ceased to be regarded as a luxury. One efficiency expert points out that it takes 15 minutes to load a day's dishes, and 73 minutes to wash them by hand. Do not, however, depend on getting large pots and pans, plastics (unless heat-resistant), or wooden or anodized aluminum pieces done well in your dishwasher. You will also have to be cautious with fine glass and china, and knives whose blades are cemented into their handles.

Before you buy a dishwasher, check your water supply. Efficient operation of a washer, depending on its size, requires from 7 to 13 gallons of water at 140°F to 160°F per load, and water pressure of about 15 to 125 pounds per square inch. Because of this requirement, you may discover that you need a model with a built-in booster heater. The capacities of dishwashers range from 5 to 18 table settings. To get the right size for you, consider not only how big your family is, but also how often you entertain. It is more economical in terms of water and electricity to run a full load every time you use your washer. Since more and more states are placing controls on the use of certain detergents, be sure that the dishwasher you buy works with a solution approved in your home state.

Ranges. The standard one-unit range-and-oven is only one of many cooking appliances these days. Now you can get counter-top burners, separate wall ovens, and many variations of built-in or cabinet-type ranges. Ranges also come with many special features, such as self-cleaning ovens, automatic timers, and clock controls. Each of these adds to the cost, so you'll have to decide which is important to you. Consider also the cooking capacity that you will need. Four burners are usually adequate, but special needs might call for six.

Gas burners heat up faster, and make high-to-low adjustments quicker. Proponents of electricity, however, say that it's cleaner,

For routine household purchases, whether for yourself or for a gift, remember to check the prices at several stores before you buy. Many large stores have their own brand label on an amazing variety of goods, and it is always worth taking a good look at these own-brand products: frequently you'll find that you can get very good quality at a lower price.

and allows more automatic devices. The danger of leaks makes it risky to buy a secondhand gas range as a general rule, unless it has been thoroughly checked and reconditioned by a reputable dealer. You should consider installation charges as part of the cost when deciding on either a used gas or electric range.

Air Conditioners. The standard criterion for measuring the power of air conditioners is the British Thermal Unit, which is the most dependable guide to cooling capacity. For most average sized rooms, 6000 to 8000 BTU's, operating on 115-120 volt AC current, is adequate. Check the noise level of the air conditioner, and see if its filters are easy to clean. A thermostat on the machine may be an added expense, but will usually pay off because automatic cutoff will save money on operating costs.

Models advertised as portable are seldom light enough to carry easily, and may present installation problems. Don't neglect to find out if installation is included in the price, and what servicing you can expect from the seller. Cooling without adequate dehumidifying will not give you the comfort you are seeking, so be sure the dehumidifying unit works well.

For worthwhile savings on new brand-name appliances, shop at discount stores. As in everything else in the money-saving game, there are some guides to wise discount shopping.

First of all, discount houses have a full share of sharp dealers out to make a fast dollar, at your expense if that's the way the profit lies. So, take your business to a store that has been around your area for some years. Visit the store to make sure it carries standard brands, and compare the prices with regular shops. Don't be let down by the helter-skelter look of most discount shops; part of the savings you get comes from the lack of fancy displays.

Next, you have to know that discount dealers sell either last year's models, or this year's surplus. This is why they can sell their merchandise at lower prices. In both cases, however, the merchandise is new, and carries a full factory warranty.

Now here's a tip on technique. Read the reports on the appliance you want to buy in the annual *Consumer Reports Buying Guide*, at the library if you don't own a copy. Make a list of several models that are rated at the performance level and quality you want. Take this list to the store with you, and buy according to it. You may not find your first-choice model, but chances are you'll find one of the names on your list. If *Consumer Reports* recommends an off-brand, you might take a chance on it; but this is not advisable unless the manufacturer's service center is convenient.

Shop the discount store way for all major appliances, carpeting, and, occasionally, furniture. Discount buying does take care, and certainly isn't as easy as strolling around a comfortable department store; but it can result in your getting a good buy at a savings of many dollars.

Buying a Car

Did you know that owning and operating a car eats up 10 to 15 per cent of your income? Knowing that, you'll realize that a car is one of the biggest buys you'll ever make. Therefore, it is well to shop carefully, and to refuse to take what doesn't suit you in every respect. Probably the first question you ask yourself when you go to buy a car is: "Should it be new or used?" There are advantages and disadvantages to each.

One advantage of a used car has to do with *depreciation*. It's a sad fact that the value of a new car diminishes drastically in its very first year, no matter what kind of treatment you give it. In fact, the minute you drive a car out of the showroom, it becomes "used", and is worth 25 to 30 per cent less than the total on the sales slip you got five minutes before. This drop in value is what is called depreciation. If you buy a used car, it is the previous owner—not you —who suffers the sharp first-year loss in its value.

In addition to savings on depreciation,

Small Appliances

Many small appliances last for years and years: use these tips to buy wisely and you can be reasonably sure of years of good service from an appliance chosen to meet your needs.

GARBAGE DISPOSERS

▶ A heavy-duty one costs somewhat more, but is cheaper in the long run because it will require fewer repairs.

▶ Find out if disposers are legal in your area before buying.

▶ If you have a septic tank, be sure it has at least a 500-gallon capacity to support a disposer.

▶ This convenient equipment is inexpensive to run.

SEWING MACHINES

▶ You can expect about 24 years of use out of most sewing machines; how much you pay does not seem to matter.

▶ Buy a well-known brand in order to get parts and servicing easily.

▶ Portables are cheaper, but you won't get full use of one if you don't leave it out permanently.

▶ If you have a portable, make a cloth dust cover yourself and save the expense of a case.

▶ A zig-zag attachment, instead of a zig-zag machine, is a great savings; it will serve for most ordinary sewing needs.

▶ Try any machine out for a few days before you decide to buy it.

▶ Make sure any machine will work on heavy fabric, such as denim.

▶ A built-in light is important; also a bobbin that is easy to fill, put in, and take out.

VACUUM CLEANERS

▶ Upright models are more efficient on rugs than tank, or canister, models.

▶ Attachments usually don't cost extra on tanks, and are easier to attach; but be sure the attachments lock in.

▶ If you don't have much rug area, you can probably save by buying an economy tank model for as little as $30 to $50.

▶ If two models work the same, but have different attachments, buy the cheaper one; you can buy other attachments later if they prove necessary for special jobs.

▶ Factory rebuilt vacuums cost less; however, be sure to buy from a factory authorized dealer.

▶ Make sure the dust bag can be removed easily.

▶ A light adds to the cost, but is usually not much needed.

Tips on Kitchenware

Whether you're starting out from scratch, filling in your supply, or replacing what's worn out, you'll make better buys using these tips.

POTS AND PANS

▶ You don't save by buying cheap pans; they often use more fuel, ruin food by scorching, and chip easily when cleaned.

▶ Aluminum and copper have the greatest heating efficiency.

▶ Good quality aluminum should be heavy; 14 to 18 *gauge* aluminum will give you almost a lifetime of service.

▶ Waterless cooking saves on fuel, but you don't need to buy special cookware; use any 8-10 gauge aluminum, or heavy copper-bottom stainless steel pots with tight-fitting covers.

STAINLESS STEEL TABLEWARE

▶ True stainless has at least 11.5 per cent chromium in it for corrosion resistance; all American stainless steel meets this standard, but much that is foreign produced does not.

▶ Better quality stainless tableware is thicker at points of stress, tapered in other places for good looks and balance; for example, a well-made knife blade will be thickest where it joins the handle, thinner at the edge and point.

▶ Look for a smooth finish on fork tines and spoon edges; test by running your finger along the edges for roughness.

▶ Good stainless never requires polishing, lasts indefinitely.

DISHES

▶ Porcelain looks more delicate, but doesn't chip or break as easily as heavier earthenware.

▶ Semiporcelain (earthenware fired to a hard glaze) is cheaper than porcelain, and wears well.

▶ Dinnerware with decorations applied under the glaze is cheaper; the decorations will also last longer.

▶ Fancy designs not only add to the cost, but also could hide flaws in the material.

▶ Look for even color, and make sure dishes are not warped.

▶ Tiny pinholes in the surface is a sign that the china is of poor quality.

▶ Best grade of plastic for dinnerware is molded melamine, which must meet government standards for thickness and weight; it costs more than semiporcelain.

Tips on Household Linen

You spend a lot of money over the years on basic household linens, even though you often replace things piece by piece to keep expenditure down. Keep these tips in mind when you go out to buy such necessaries as sheets, towels, and blankets. They'll help you get better buys.

TOWELS

▶ Plain white towels are cheapest and most absorbent.

▶ Dark colors not only cost more, but also fade more, and take extra care because of need for being washed separately.

▶ Look for thick, long loops of double thread for better absorbency.

▶ Plain weave wears better than raised design.

SHEETS

▶ You pay more for pastel colors; you pay most for prints.

▶ Combed cotton wears better, but doesn't always cost more.

▶ If you have sheets laundered, the lighter percale ones will save on laundry bills.

▶ Buy by thread count: 140-148 is high for muslin; 186-190 is medium for percale; both are usually good buys in sales.

▶ Hold a piece of the sheet up to the light and look for the following as a measure of strength:
1. vertical and horizontal threads of the same thickness
2. even weaving
3. no thin spots
4. no knots in the material

BLANKETS

▶ Look at part of the blanket through the light; if you see that the weave is loose, don't buy.

▶ Good synthetic blankets are better all-around buys than cheap wool ones.

▶ Pluck at the nap to be sure it's firm.

▶ Better blankets should have 7- or 8-inch nylon binding.

▶ Wool is warmest, but takes more care in cleaning and storing.

▶ Blankets of 75 to 80 per cent wool are cheaper, and as warm as all-wool ones; any smaller percentage of wool means that the blankets are not a good buy, however.

▶ Rayon is less warm, wears less well, and is dangerous because it's inflammable.

Rise in Car Ownership

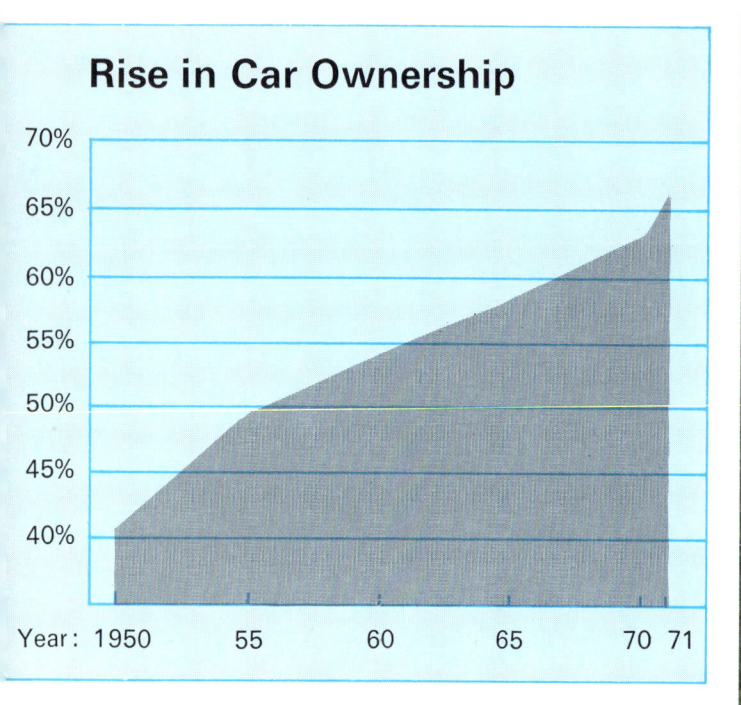

(Graph showing car ownership percentage rising from about 41% in 1950 to about 65% in 1971.)

Above: the statistics tell the tale that car ownership in the United States increases year by year. Among the many families that have private cars, a good number own two—and some even three.

Right and below: the spanking new cars roll off the assembly line, and millions of excited families climb in for the most expensive ride they'll ever take—the block away from the agency. In just those few minutes, their brand new car becomes a used car, and drops hundreds of dollars in value. Besides this depreciation, cars are a continuous and hefty expense to a family, as can be seen from the figures on what it costs to operate a car for one year.

the greatest single advantage of a used car is, of course, the lower initial cost. On the debit side, however, repairs are usually needed more frequently, and guarantees and warranties—if any at all—are more limited than for new cars.

Used cars are not necessarily bargains on another count. They may have major weaknesses from having been driven hard and maintained poorly. Yet such weaknesses can be concealed beneath a gleaming exterior of new paint or wax. Therefore, when you find a used car you like, you should have a mechanic examine it thoroughly before you make a final decision to buy it. If you have a regular mechanic and are a good customer, he may check over one or

Car Costs for a Year

Cost heading	Cost in dollars	% of total
Depreciation	732	48.9
Insurance	302	20.1
License and registration	27	1.8
Gasoline and oil	279	18.6
Maintenance	71	4.7
Tires	54	3.6
Miscellaneous expense (parking, tolls, etc.)	35	2.3
Total annual outlay	$1,500	100.0

Note: costs shown here are based on typical use of a medium-priced, four-door sedan with an 8-cylinder engine, automatic transmission, and power steering. Annual mileage is estimated at about 10,000. The percentages also assume that you trade in your car at the end of the third year of use.

Source: "Personal Money Management" American Bankers Association, 1970 two cars free. Otherwise, you will probably have to pay a flat fee of about $25 to $30 for a mechanic's service, which is well worth it.

If you don't know a mechanic whose judgment you trust, you should try to find an auto diagnostic clinic. More and more of them are springing up in urban centers around the country. For $25 or so, they will check about 75 potential trouble spots in a car. The best of these clinics are the ones that do checkups only, without operating a repair service of their own.

One bit of help to you is a new federal law that went into effect in early 1973. Under this law, sellers must certify that the mileage shown on the car's *odometer* (not speedometer—that mainly measures miles-per-hour) is accurate to the best of their knowledge. The law also prohibits disconnecting or resetting odometers except for needed repairs. In that case, the repairman must set the mileage at zero, and post a notice on the left door frame telling what the mileage was before the repair. It is unlawful to remove or alter the repairman's notice in any way.

With the law making it easier for you to check the mileage of a used car, you can also make some other quick checks yourself. See the diagram on pages 76-77 for tips on what to look out for.

After adding it all up, you decide there are more minuses than pluses in buying a used car. That brings you to a new car. What, then, for the wary buyer?

Trade-in or Do-it-Yourself Sale
You probably plan to get rid of the car you have now, and use the money for a down payment on the new wheels. Lest you fall victim to trade-in traps, find out for yourself in advance what the fair market value of your car is. Two of a host of sources of used car prices are the *Consumer Reports Buying Guide,* which comes out at the end of each year, and the *Blue Book,* which is published monthly by auto dealers' associations. Most banks and savings and loan associations have a *Blue Book* that you can look at; in it you will find the prices of cars from one to six years old. *Blue Book* prices, being average market values, are nothing more than a guide. You may be able to do better. On the other hand, if your car has a few fender wrinkles, and doesn't hum when it's switched on, you may do worse.

As a general rule, you will almost always be ahead by selling your car to a private buyer rather than trading it in to a dealer. This calls for a certain amount of effort and bother you may not want to undertake, especially since you can't tell when a buyer will happen by.

One way to make good savings on a car is simply to wait until the right time to buy. In August and September, when the new models begin coming off the assembly lines, dealers get the itch to clear out their showrooms of whatever they might have on hand. Consequently, they are willing to lop a few dollars off last year's models for the sake of a fast sale at that time. Also, manufacturers offer their dealers rebates of about five per cent on the old models. On a $3000 car, this amounts to about $150. You should ask for at least the amount of this rebate as a reduction in the price to you. Even if you are after one of the new models, restrain yourself until the winter months, when better prices are usually to be had.

Restraint in general may be the key word to successful car buying. If you could

You don't have to be an expert to pick a sound used car: just drive it around to a mechanic you trust and let him do the checking. But as he'll almost certainly charge you for the job, you can do some checking yourself beforehand by using these guidelines.

Stand 10 to 15 feet away from the car in a good light. Watch to see whether the light catches any bumps or dents in the surface. Such irregularities very often mean that the car has been in a major accident. Look too for weld marks in the frame of the car, or have a mechanic check for them. These show that the car has been in a bad accident, and are good grounds for rejecting it without further examination.

Check That Used Car!

Look for rust at the bottom of fenders, around the head and tail lights, and along the bottom of door and body. Small blisters in the paint are sure signs of rust underneath. You should refuse at once any car that is too rusted.

Check to see that the wheels are straight — first when the car is standing still, then when it is driven directly away from you. If you find the wheels are headed in slightly different directions, pass up the car immediately.

Let the car's engine warm up for at least 15 minutes. Then pull up the oil dip stick. If the oil looks white, or is filled with white bubbles, this probably means the car's cooling system is leaking into the engine block; and this means a major problem.

Check the exhaust by holding a matchbook cover over the tail pipe. It should flap in a steady rhythm. Also, look out for wisps of blue smoke, both while the engine is idling and when it is raced. Black smoke is a sign that the gas is of too rich a mix. This fault can usually be corrected by a simple adjustment of the carburetor.

When you test drive the car, turn a few corners sharply. The steering wheel should work smoothly, without squeaks, groans, or shimmying. Make sure you test drive the car over a rough, potholed road. If there are any defects in the body and suspension, this test will show them up.

To test the brakes, first press the pedal down while the car is immobile. If the pedal goes almost to the floor, this means the car probably needs new brake shoes. When you are test driving, accelerate to about 45 mph and brake suddenly. Squealing or pulling brakes may mean a minor problem, but sudden swerving or grabbing are always warnings that serious repairs will be needed. The emerging brake on the car should be checked by halting on a steep hill. If the brake fails to hold, this may mean only minor adjustment—but it could also indicate major trouble.

Check the car's engine by accelerating suddenly from about 20 to 55 mph. This may be a strain on the engine, but even so it should not buck, hesitate, or miss. Another good engine test is to accelerate from slow to moderate speed while driving up a steep hill. The motor should pull easily.

restrain yourself from buying most of the optional equipment, you could save up to $100 to $300. Such a stripped model would have to be ordered for you, however, so it takes patience as well as restraint to make this kind of savings.

The Art of Bargaining
Knowing just what a reasonable price might be is the key to smart bargaining with car dealers. Your first bit of valuable bargaining ammunition is the knowledge that the dealer paid from 20 to 30 per cent less than the sticker price, which is the cost of the basic model with all required safety equipment. It also helps you to know that most dealers consider $250 to $300 an adequate profit.

Take a full-size standard model of a medium priced car, for example. The sticker price will probably be around $3500. Subtract 25 per cent of that, or $875, and you have $2625 as the price the dealer paid. To this, add $250 as the dealer's profit, and your total is $2875. (If you can get a much lower deal than that, you don't need bargaining tips from anyone.) For a small car, do the same exercise using 20 per cent, and for a big car, calculate at 30 per cent.

Don't forget that extras are worth bargaining for just as much as the basic car—especially since they are usually marked up as much as 30 to 40 per cent. You should be able to bargain about 15 per cent off the price of such extras as power brakes, power steering, radio, and air conditioning.

To get even more bargaining power, play one dealer against another. Boldly tell Dealer A that Dealer B will give you a bigger discount. It often happens that Dealer A wants the sale badly enough to meet, or beat, the other offer.

It's wise to buy a make of automobile that can be serviced near home.

Watch Those Gimmicks
When buying a new car, choosing a reputable dealer is all-important. More often than not, you will return to him later for repairs or trade-ins, so the sale is only the beginning of a long relationship. A call to your Better Business Bureau is never a bad idea. The bureau can steer you clear of the known shady dealers, and can also warn you about some of the sales gimmicks that you should guard against.

One ruse of disreputable salesmen is to quote you a price they have no intention of making good on. Since the price is genuinely low, you will eagerly and unsuspectingly sign a sales contract, and begin looking forward to the day your new car is delivered. All too often, this day never comes. Just before delivery time, you get a call from the salesman, who says his boss just won't let him sell the car for such a low price, and if you don't come up with an additional $200 or $300, you will not get the car. Unfortunately, it is perfectly legal for salesmen to back out like this. The purchase orders used by all car dealers contain a clause saying the deal is not binding until an officer of the firm, as well as the salesman, approves it. No reputable dealer, however, will resort to this kind of trick to make a sale. The Better Business Bureau has adopted a code saying that the customer must be notified within two working days if his order is rejected. Reputable dealers follow this code.

Another tip on dealing with dealers: if you plan to pay cash for the car, keep it quiet until the dealer writes up the sales check. It's a hard fact of our credit way of life that many car dealers hate cash transactions, because they often make as much, or more, on finance charges as on the sale. When a dealer learns you will arrive to pick up your car with a check (it might be advisable to get a certified one), he may be hopping mad, and may try to call off the deal. That's why it is important to have the sales slip already in your hand. Let the dealer rave. You have a right to be a cash customer. If you buy on credit in the more usual way, beware of the dealer who offers financing, or suggests a loan agency. You usually pay through the nose for this kind of credit.

Above: used car salesmen—like any other group of businessmen—range from responsible to crooked. But even the best of them make their money by selling you on a used car—fast. So keep your wits about you while listening to a sales talk, and don't be pressured into a quick decision.

Right: take a critical, careful look at the car outside and in, and then go home to think about it before you decide. Remember that although each used car is, by definition, unique, people trade cars in every day, and if you miss one treasure, you'll almost certainly find another next week.

Your Bargain Calendar

January

Traditionally a great month for bargains in towels, sheets, and other white goods, but did you know that it's also a good time to buy drugs and cosmetics, furniture, floor coverings, and home furnishings generally, cruisewear, lingerie, and furs?

February

China, glass, silver, men's shirts, mattresses, and bedding generally are the chief bargains to go hunting for in February. Many big stores run furniture and houseware sales through February too, so this can be the month to buy those household items you've been meaning to purchase for ages and just never got around to. February can be a good month to buy a new ca

May

House furnishings, outdoor furniture, luggage, all these are good May buys. But May is also the time for spring cleaning, and many stores have specials on the polishes, mops, and other things you'll need for all those chores. This can be a good time too for looking at carpets and rugs, which can often have their prices cut about now.

June

Best bargains this month are in the furniture department, because stores are making way for the semiannual models that are about to come in. But keep your eyes open for anything you need—for now or later in the year—in the way of bedding, hosiery and lingerie, women's shoes and clothes for the men and boys in your family

September

Look out for September sales of china and house furnishings. And if you can wait until the end of the month to set up your children in back-to-school wear, you can find some really good bargains—though be warned, you may not find exactly what you want in all sizes.

October

Variety is the keynote this month—major household appliances like refrigerators, freezers, TV, and so on; evening wear; outerwear; silverware; home furnishings—all these can be available at discount. And if your husband is an angling fanatic, this is the time to watch out for end-of-season bargains in rods and reels.

Everybody loves a bargain, but today it's almost a necessity to get bargains in order to keep up with the cost of living. This calendar shows when certain merchandise is generally put on sale by retailers. If you buy the things you want only in the months they are reduced, you can save money year around on most personal and household goods.

March

New cars are still good value now in many showrooms, but March is also a good month for buying garden tools and supplies, and fabrics of all kinds in many stores. There are also special sales and pre-season promotions for both men's and women's clothing. Skis and skates too can be a good buy as the spring approaches.

April

Sales follow on the heels of Easter in much the same way as they come with a rush after Christmas. Fabrics, lingerie, hosiery, and women's shoes all rank high on the good buy list. Late April is a good time for men's and boy's suits and women's dresses and hats.

July

Furniture is still cheaper at a good number of stores in July, and likewise fabrics and furs. Summer goods are also being cleared to make room for fall goods—which means you can often pick up bargains in air conditioners, garden supplies, summer sports equipment and sportswear, and men's summer suits.

August

August can be a good time for buying a car, because this is the clearance time on current models. And any summer goods not marked down in July are likely to be cheap this month—things like summer furniture, lawnmowers, camping equipment, and other yard tools and vacation equipment. Buy now for next summer!

November

Christmas is coming, so shop now and beat the rush. But if you can spare the time—and cash—this, believe it or not, is a good month for seasonal buys in women's winter coats, woolen dresses, and men's suits. Why? Because many stores are simply trying to make room for their second consignments of these items.

December

This is a bleak time in the sales calendar, as both stores and shoppers concentrate upon the real business of Christmas shopping. The few exceptions are to be found predictably in the resort and cruisewear departments, and more surprisingly in car showrooms, where salesmen find so few customers they may well be ready to offer reductions to make a sale.

Home Buying and Renting

5

After two rent increases in three years, and under the threat of another one, Jane and Joe Freeman have decided to become homeowners. They know that owning a house in a good neighborhood is one of the more certain hedges against inflation. Besides, Jane is now pregnant, so their small city apartment will soon be too cramped.

The Freemans did a lot of dreaming and planning over the winter, and have a clear idea of the area they'd like to live in, the price they can afford to pay, and the kind of house they want. Jane has beautiful visions of a large, sunny kitchen; Joe is already thinking of do-it-yourself projects in his first home workshop.

The couple started to house-hunt seriously in early spring, and the experience wasn't as much fun as they had thought it would be. A spell of cold, rainy weather turned new developments into a sea of mud, and made older communities seem dreary and unwelcoming. Finally a sunny day came. The world seemed gloriously green, and the real estate agent had "just the house" for them. "It's about eight years old," he said, "but it's in fine condition, and the property value in the area is bound to stay up."

The garden of the house was a delight, ablaze with daffodils and tulips. Both Jane and Joe fell in love with it at first sight. True, the house was not as roomy as they had wanted and the attic was hardly insulated, but there was a big, bright kitchen, and plenty of room in the basement for a workshop. Everything seemed to check out, the owner was cheerful and friendly, giving them tips about the garden, and Joe was naturally anxious to get Jane settled in a new home

It's great fun looking at a house for sale—looking around the rooms you can imagine what it would be like to live there (and yellow curtains at that window would be lovely). But don't get carried away: you're on the edge of the biggest expenditure you're likely to make.

Whether you like your spot of green to be right in the middle of the city, or whether you love the sound of the birds early on a country morning, or hope to find a suburban paradise somewhere in between, the kind of life you want to lead will play a big part in determining where your family lives.

before she had the baby. They agreed to buy the house, and went home that afternoon happily discussing how they would arrange the furniture.

Here are the Freemans a year later, sadder but wiser, as the saying goes. First, they have learned that the owner could have been—and expected to be—bargained down a few thousand dollars. Second, the heating bills have been much higher than anticipated because of the uninsulated roof, and the necessity to keep the house extra warm for the baby. Not only that, the one room suitable for a nursery had turned out to be next to the living room. Any time the television is on it wakes the baby, who tries to drown out the noise with his cries. Jane's sunny kitchen was shaded all summer by the leaves on the trees outside, and the sun did little to offset the cold drafts from the windows in the winter.

The list goes on. Joe's workshop is poorly lit, and noisy when the furnace is on. And it flooded during heavy summer rains, and ruined $50 worth of wood. Perhaps the worst thing of all, though, was that the septic tank had to be replaced by a connection to the city sewer. That had cost them $400, increased their taxes, and ruined a large slice of their lawn and beloved flower beds. The garden, by the way, proved too much for Jane to handle.

Actually, the Freemans were comparatively lucky. The unexpected $400 expense will turn into an asset in the long run, because the sewer connection is an improvement that increases the property value. The connection may also be a long-run money-saver because it eliminates forever the periodic problems with septic tanks. Furthermore, although the Freemans had bought mostly on impulse, without more than a token inspection of the house, and with little idea of what home-owning involves, they didn't have any major disasters. They could have been afflicted with termites, a leaky roof, a plumbing system breakdown, or any one of a number of calamities that can befall the new and unwary homeowner.

Selecting a house is a difficult process, and considering the amount of financial and emotional strain it can bring, you should learn all you can about it before you even pick up the classifieds. After all, you wouldn't buy an expensive dress without first trying it on.

How You Want to Live

As you read this you're probably sitting snugly in a home you love. But what if you find out shortly that you'll have to move to a new town because of your husband's promotion or transfer? Or your soon-to-be-married son asks advice about home ownership? Or your best friend, single again after a divorce, wants to talk over her altered living needs? You'll be thinking about the housing problem as though you were starting out anew, so it's well to examine the options.

Naturally, your anticipated lifestyle will have a lot to do with your choice of a home. You may want a downtown apartment with its convenience to shops, restaurants, and entertainment. You may prefer an apartment or house on the outskirts of town for more quiet without being too far from the

85

First Check the Neighborhood

The neighborhood you move into will be just as important as the house you live in, so before you decide, look over these questions and make sure you have satisfactory answers to them. Honeysuckle curling over the porch is pretty, but convenient schools for the kids are important.

TAXES
▶ Are the taxes higher or lower than those in similar areas? Find out about special assessments as well as real estate taxes, but don't be put off by relatively high ones. The important thing is to learn how the tax money is used, and if it is going into making a better community, it could be worth it.

SCHOOLS
▶ Is the local school building in good condition, and does it have an adequate library, gym, cafeteria, and playground?
▶ Are the students on double session? If not now, are classes getting so big that double sessions might be put into effect?
▶ Are there special teachers for music, languages, science, math, and art? Look also for a guidance counselor, nurse, and psychologist.
▶ Does the school budget show community support? Find out if parents are satisfied with the superintendent and school board, and if they vote budget increases when necessary.
▶ Is the PTA well organized and active? You can get a general feeling about the school by talking to a few members.

PUBLIC SERVICES
▶ Are fire and police protection good? Fire departments are rated by the American Insurance Association, and the rating should be available to you at the town hall. A scale rating of 4 is average for big cities, 5 for smaller towns. The size of the police department in comparison with nearby communities will tell you something about its adequacy. If property owners have no complaints, it's a good sign.
▶ Is garbage collection free? If not, are private fees high?
▶ Is the water system safe, and is the water too hard? Find out the bacteria count; it should be negative. Very hard water causes scaling inside hot water pipes, and may stain laundry.
▶ Are you near a bank, post office, hospital? These services are convenient—and the hospital may be needed in an emergency. You might also look for a neighborhood movie.

GENERAL CONVENIENCE

▶ Will you have to drive to work? Make a test run to see how long the journey is door-to-door. Take into account the amount of traffic, toll costs if any, parking near work.

▶ Is there public transportation for commuting? How long will it take door-to-door, and what will it cost? If you have to use your car to get to the station, and pay for parking there, it can be expensive.

▶ Is the nearest shopping place a car ride away? You may not like this if you need only a loaf of bread or quart of milk and there is no store near.

▶ Can you easily get home from town after rush hour service is over? Check whether the evening and late night service is adequate.

ZONING REGULATIONS

▶ Does the zoning law allow industrial development near you? Is a heavy-traffic highway being planned? Neither of these is desirable. Try asking local shopkeepers about rumors of coming industry, roads, or apartment developments.

▶ Will local restrictions prevent you from building the kind of house you want? Talk to the building inspector. Often there are regulations against prefabs and contemporary designs, or against making additions later.

STABILITY OF NEIGHBORHOOD

▶ Are there any multiple dwellings, such as rooming or boarding houses? Except for college communities, where students are transient residents by the nature of things, rooming and boarding houses usually foretell a decaying area.

▶ Are there a lot of school-age children around This is a good sign of stability, because most families try to stay in one neighborhood till the children finish school.

▶ Does the community have good parks and libraries? These and other recreational facilities help make a neighborhood stable, and also add to a fuller life.

center of things. You may decide to forsake the town altogether for a house either in the suburbs or the country.

Rent or Buy?
Whether you decide to live in an apartment or a house, you are still left with the decision of buying or renting.

Remember that renting doesn't necessarily mean you are limited to an apartment. You can rent houses, too. Likewise, buying doesn't always mean you have to live in a house. You can buy apartments, too. Consider the following pros and cons before making the important decision about whether to rent or buy.

Renting is ideal for singles and newlyweds who want to be free to move about, or to try out different lifestyles before settling down. It is also financially suited to their pocket-books, because no large down payment is necessary. Also monthly expenses are fairly well fixed and easy to budget, because all you have to plan for are the rent and utilities payments. There's no worry about repairing the furnace, mowing the lawn, shoveling the driveway, or having any other unexpected household expenses or chores cut into your social life or your budget. On the other hand, you'll probably have limited freedom to remodel or redecorate—meaning that you'll just have to live with the ghastly tiles in the bathroom. Apartments can also be noisy, crowded, and have little or no place for children to play.

Good Sense in Renting
If renting turns out to be your choice—or necessity—chances are you'll end up with an apartment. In that case, the following tips on sensible renting should be a help. If it's a house you're renting, things are a bit more complicated. However, just take the advice on apartment renting, throw in some common sense, and you should be able to come up with a good strategy.

Looking for an apartment usually involves enough walking and stairs climbing to put an Olympic team in shape. You'll start either by reading and following up newspaper ads—making phone calls or ringing doorbells—or by contacting a real estate agent, who will do some of these chores for you. The agent will probably have lists of apartments of the type you're looking for, and may know of some that aren't advertised. Real estate agencies can also be valuable in giving you information about zoning laws, the safety of the neighborhood, and the kind of people living there. Don't count on an

Rent or Buy: Cost Comparison

Item	Apartment Renting	House owning
Mortgage interest/rent payment	$162.50	$90.20
Payment toward principle/savings	61.00	61.00
Taxes	—	31.20
Fire and liability insurance	—	6.50
Fuel	—	26.00
Electricity	13.00	13.00
Water	—	6.50
Garbage pickup	—	4.00
Lost interest	—	25.00
Maintenance	—	45.00
Totals	$236.50	$320.90

Right: apartment living, which doesn't demand the enormous initial financial commitment of house-buying, and offers freedom from homeowner responsibilities, suits many mobile Americans the best.

Below right: the extra room to stretch out in, the long-term advantages of home ownership, and the satisfaction of owning the roof overhead lead the typical family to buy a house.

Below left: buying a house is certainly more expensive than renting in terms of the monthly expenditure, but most people consider it worthwhile in the long run.

agent to volunteer much information, however. His job is to rent or sell property. So you had better prepare a checklist of questions to ask him.

A rundown appearance of an apartment is a warning that a slow or uncooperative landlord is behind the scenes. Make sure the place isn't a fire trap, and that you have a fire escape you don't have to be a monkey to use. While you're checking how easily you can get out, also notice how easy it is for others to get in. Doors, windows, and skylights should be strong and burglar-proof. Finally, find out whether a janitor lives on the premises to take care of both normal maintenance and emergency repairs.

If the apartment is furnished, think about whether the furniture provided is adequate and reasonably attractive. Is there a bathtub when you prefer a shower? Is the location on the dreary, sunless north side of the building? Is the kitchen equipment and all plumbing in good working condition? These are a few questions you should ask. Others will occur to you, based on your personal tastes and circumstances. Satisfy yourself on the answers before you sign any lease.

One other note about renting. Financial experts say you should spend no more than one week's take-home pay on a month's rent.

Buying—and What to Buy
If owning a home of your own appeals to you, there are sound, practical reasons for buying rather than renting. You know that your monthly mortgage payments, unlike rent, are leading up to something tangible: home and property ownership. You know the sense of security that comes with owning the roof over your head. And it's sound economics for you to think in terms of the tax deductions you can get on the interest you pay on a mortgage (you get no such deductions on rent), and of the protection home ownership gives against inflation.

If these and other considerations make you decide on buying, your first thought will probably be a house. There are other alternatives of ownership, though, and you

Condominiums, like these three in Colorado, Florida, and Oregon, are an interesting option for people not needing the spaciousness of a house, but wanting the financial advantages of home ownership, or for those wanting a second home in the place the family spends vacations.

won't be amiss to give them some serious consideration. What about a condominium, cooperative apartment, or mobile home? Each of these has special advantages that you may not be aware of—and one could turn out to suit you to a T.

For instance, a condominium or cooperative apartment gives the advantages of apartment living combined with the benefits of ownership—but minus size, private grounds, and a certain freedom of action. Either is usually fine for a small family, a retired couple, or those who want a permanent vacation home in a resort area.

In each case, a group of owner-tenants band together to form an association that is collectively responsible for the maintenance of the property. Most condominiums and co-ops are apartment buildings, either singly or in a development. They often have private recreation facilities, and sometimes have community rooms. The board of directors hires grounds keepers and maintenance men, and tenants pay a share of the costs. You can rent your apartment to others while you are away, or just let it sit empty, knowing that it is being looked after. Of course, as a homeowner, you are eligible for certain income tax deductions.

There is one big difference between a co-op and a condominium. In a co-op you purchase stock in the owner-tenants' corporation. You therefore own a portion of the entire property, and are entitled to live in the portion that is your apartment. There is only one mortgage on the whole place, so you foot a share of the payments each month —plus some more for taxes, insurance, maintenance, and anything else looked after by the board of directors. It's just as though you and your friends all chipped in to buy a yacht, and hired a crew to sail and take care of it for you.

If you have an apartment in a condo-

91

minium, however, you own your set of rooms, as though they were out in the woods, in one unit, five miles from your nearest neighbor. You therefore have your individual and separate mortgage and taxes. However, since you are squeezed together with your neighbors, you naturally get together on maintenance, heating, grounds and driveways, swimming pools, and anything else you share. Just as in a co-op, the board of directors hires a maintenance staff for the building and grounds, and you help pay for it by an annual fee.

Mobile Homes and Trailers
The first thing you should know about mobile homes and trailers is the difference between the two. A mobile home isn't really very mobile, and a trailer is mobile without being much of a home. Trailers are great for vacationers, or for childless or retired couples hopelessly bitten by the travel bug. Mobile homes look a bit like trailers in basic design, but they go nowhere except on the exact site you've chosen. Mobile homes are usually mobile only once during their lifetime. Thereafter they are tied down, hooked up, expanded out, decorated in, and landscaped around to the point that no one would ever dream of disturbing them again.

The prices of mobile homes range between

Houses come in an amazing variety of styles and sizes, some far more suitable for your way of living than others. If you're house hunting in an area where the seasons are markedly different, imagine what the house will be like in the various seasons—will bare trees allow no privacy in winter, for example?

$4000 and $20,000. The most expensive models are often two separate trailers that are put together at the permanent location to form a sizeable dwelling. Furnishings, major appliances, and towing fees are generally included in the buying price. Although down payments are lower than for houses, financing is often done through the dealer, which means higher interest rates. Recently, however, banks and other lenders have come around to financing mobile homes. The Federal Housing Authority (FHA) and Veterans Administration (VA), the two government agencies active in granting housing loans, are also making loans available for mobile homes.

Local regulations and town ordinances are often strict about where you can put your mobile home, so you may end up in a less-than-beautiful trailer park. Take into consideration that you'll have to rent a site for $30 to $100 a month, and that children and pets may not be allowed. Guard yourself against badly built mobile homes by making sure yours is built according to the standards of the American National Standards Institute.

The House For You
Finally, we get to the ordinary, everyday house, and it, too, comes in a number of varieties according to your needs. All the different types and models of homes cannot be dealt with in a limited space, but here's a brief rundown on what you should look out for in the new and the older house.

The design and layout of your new house should be attractive and efficient, and everything in it should work to perfection. One big advantage is that you don't have to redo or live with a previous owner's idea of decoration. Possible disadvantages are that new housing developments may be unfinished, treeless, and ugly. Later on, new roads and schools may be needed, and meeting the costs of these will boost your taxes. The builder, too, may be fly-by-night and go bankrupt or otherwise be unavailable when building faults show up. You can, however, protect yourself against most of these problems by buying from a well-established builder and dealing with a reputable community bank. The one thing you can't do much about is taxes—except, of course, to give your opinion by voting.

You may be enchanted with an older house because of some reminder of yesteryear—perhaps a curved staircase or a working fireplace—but beware! It will take a surprising amount of cash to rebuild basic structures, and modernize heating, plumbing, and electrical systems. The house may also be poorly laid out for modern living. In all, you may end up putting more into it than you can get back out of it, should you want to sell.

Whether you're buying a new or an *existing* home (that's the proper realty term for the almost new, older, and old house), be sure you give it a thorough going-over. In fact, it pays to have an existing house checked by a real estate appraiser, whom you can find through the phone book Yellow Pages, or the local Board of Realtors. The fee can run from $50 to $100—but it may be the smartest outlay of cash you've ever made.

Even before you thump a wall or rattle a door handle, though, you should think about location and surroundings from every possible angle. Margaret and Ted Simpson, who had two school-age youngsters, paid attention only to the house itself when they bought. The interior design was all they wanted, and inspection proved the whole house to be sound. In they moved—and out went their joy.

Ted found that he had to go to work on one of the busiest traffic routes in the area. The highway he used was disturbingly close to the house, both from the viewpoint of safety for the children, and noise. They wondered how they could have failed to notice it when first looking at the house.

Came the fall and school registration time. More woe. The school was across that dreaded highway. Moreover, there had been chronic staff problems for the last six years, and neighborhood parents were alarmed about the quality of education their children were getting.

Was that all? Unfortunately, no. A drive-in movie firm bought up the nice patch of woods bordering the Simpsons' house, and they learned too late that the zoning laws allowed it. (They could have checked on zoning regulations at the town hall.) Even their hopes for a colorful garden in bloom were shattered with the realization that their soil was rocky and poor.

It's understandable that the Simpsons wanted to pack it up. They had reason to worry, however. Could they resell the house without taking a loss?

This points up that, before buying a house, you ought to find out about shopping, transportation, schools, zoning laws, and every niggling question you can think of. (Bet you

Right: a large trailer park. If you decide on a mobile home, the park you choose will be your neighborhood, so check it out as carefully as you would if you were buying a house.

Left: Skyrise Terrace, the first multi-level mobile home project, built near St. Paul, Minnesota. It is planned to save space in an area where land costs are becoming prohibitive.

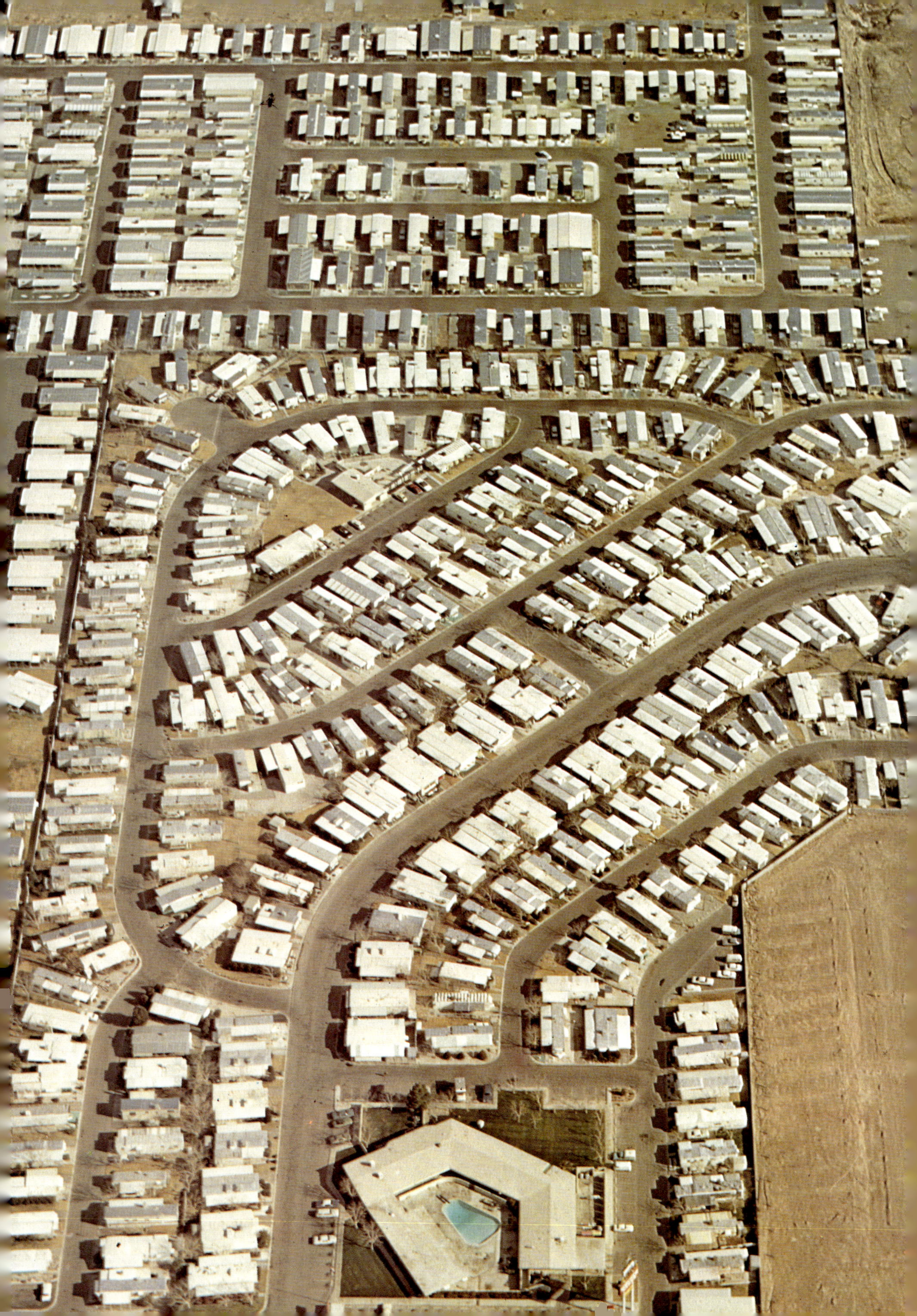

Below: to many, like this couple, there is no substitute for a custom-built home that is designed to their exact specifications—in spite of the expense, time, and often worry, that private building entails.

Right: maybe the style of this home is not to every taste, but the idea that it has been individually created by a professional architect is appealing to most people who dream of living in the perfect home.

didn't consider whether the gentle-looking river nearby floods. Or whether the site is on filled-in swamp that mosquitoes are reluctant to leave.) Once you have satisfied yourself on what's outside of the house, only then are you ready to go inside.

The first thing to consider inside is the layout of the house. A well-designed floor plan gives you a feeling of space, as well as comfort, privacy, and convenience. You should take special note of whether the living, sleeping, and working areas are separated, for this layout gives you the most satisfactory living arrangement. You might have special interest in an attic for future dorm use, or a basement for laundry facilities. Make sure they're as light and airy as possible. Examine the stairs. Are there too many, or are they too steep, for little Susie or Granny Mitchell?

The construction quality of a house is all-important. To help you look for possible trouble spots, study the diagram on page 98. It gives pointers about insulation, plumbing fixtures, electrical wiring, and other vital basics that make a sound home.

If you've asked yourself too many questions—but you know they must be asked—just go home and take a breather. Think about the interior design, about how much time and money will be required, about whether the house is that bit too far from the supermarket.

Think, too, about whether you can really afford the price. (If you follow the advice of expert economists, you should allot no

Buying an Old House?

Take a good look at what lies under the pretty face of the house you're considering: these tips give you a few questions to answer as a start. Wallpaper can be changed easily, but rewiring an old house for modern requirements can be ruinous.

PLUMBING
▶ Is the water pressure high enough? Turn on several faucets at once, upstairs and down if the house is two-story. If the pressure drops, there may be bad corrosion of the pipes.

▶ Try to flush a cigarette down the toilet; if the pressure is good, it will be pulled down at once.

▶ Do you get hot water as soon as you turn on the hot-water faucet? If not, the plumbing system may be outworn or outmoded.

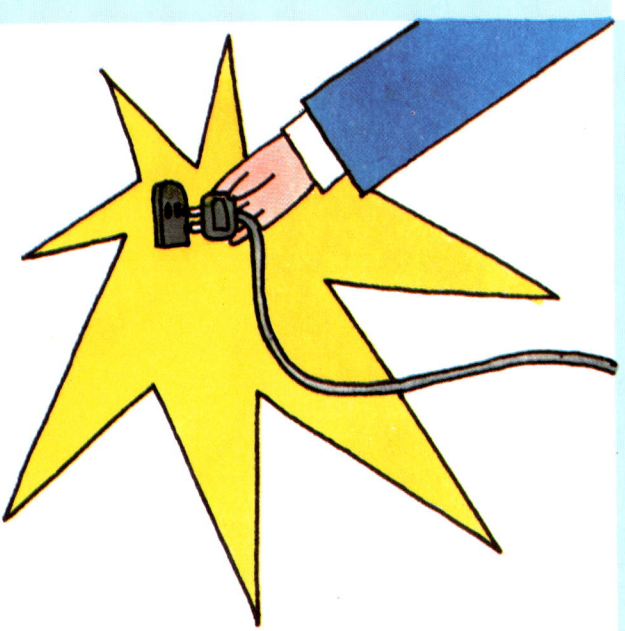

ELECTRICITY
▶ Can the present wiring carry all the appliances a modern family is likely to have? Old-fashioned 60-amp wiring won't do.

▶ Are the electrical outlets well placed, and are there enough of them?

▶ Do you see wires held to walls or framing by porcelain knobs? Take this as a warning sign that the electrical system could be inadequate and unsafe.

BASEMENT
▶ Are the foundation walls strong and sturdy? Look for cracks, crumbling, or patching.

▶ Can you see a "high-water mark"? This is a sign of flooding. If you find a sump pump hidden under a wooden hatch, beware; it could be that the flooding problem is consistent and serious.

▶ Is there an unpleasant humid smell around? This usually means trouble, and you'd better get an expert's opinion at once.

▶ Are the joists (beams supporting the upstairs floor) firm? If they are shored up in any way, find out why.

GENERAL INSIDE CONDITION

▶ Will the floors have to be sanded and finished? Worse, will patching of rotten floorboards be necessary?

▶ Are there any watermarks on the ceilings of the rooms? This is a danger signal for a leaky roof. If that roof happens to be slate, repairs are very expensive.

▶ Are the doorknobs, faucets, and other hardware in good condition?

▶ Do the stairs or floor shake when you walk heavily? If so, the house supports may be weak.

EXTERIOR

▶ Has the chimney started to separate from the house? Check this, and also if there are any broken bricks or loose mortar.

▶ Are the window sills and frames free of any rot? Look especially closely if they have been freshly painted; this may be a coverup to hide deterioration.

▶ Does the roof pass inspection? (Get a professional roofer to look it over if you can't do it yourself.) A shingle roof should have no broken or missing shingles. An asphalt composition roof should have no bubbles, peeling, or breaks.

▶ Is the flashing (protective covering at chimney and other joints) of copper, aluminum, or plastic? Other materials are not usually watertight or rustproof enough.

TERMITES

▶ Termites can bring your house tumbling down about your head, they are that destructive. Get a reputable pest control firm to make an inspection if the seller has no certificate of inspection to prove the house is termite-free.

more than 25 per cent of your monthly after-tax income for monthly housing costs. This last figure is further broken down into roughly 20 per cent for basic payments, such as mortgage, local taxes, and insurance, and the remaining 5 per cent for upkeep and maintenance.)

Happy on all the important counts? Then it is the house you want, and you're ready to buy it.

After your decision to buy, the next step toward getting an older house is to have it appraised. This will establish its real market value. With the figures supplied by the appraiser, you'll have solid facts to use in bargaining with the owner. At this point, it is a wise precaution to contact a real estate lawyer. (Your bank should be able to recommend a reliable one.) Legal advice will be invaluable in the later phases of negotiation and closure.

Coolness and a sense of timing can save you thousands of dollars in bargaining for a house. Even if you feel you lack these qualities, don't accept the asking price without some maneuvering to bring it down.

Once the price is settled, you will almost always be asked to put up a deposit, sometimes called "earnest money". The amount will vary with the price of the house—probably from several hundred to a thousand dollars. Consult your lawyer before signing an earnest money agreement to make sure you and your money are fully protected. Also be sure to get and keep a receipt for the deposit you put down on the house.

Getting a Mortgage

Now comes the part you definitely haven't been waiting for—getting a mortgage. Here's how it works. The mortgage is two things: a loan you turn over at once to buy property, and the property itself as security for the loan. Mortgages are usually granted for a long term. You should be familiar with the three basic types of mortgages: the FHA, the VA, and the conventional mortgage.

The FHA is a government agency, but the government itself does not lend money. The FHA guarantees loans made by private lenders. A VA mortgage is available only to armed forces veterans of World War II and of later conflicts. Although in special circumstances the VA itself will make a direct loan, the money must in most cases come from a conventional lender. The VA, like the FHA, then guarantees the loan in case of the veteran's death or default on payments.

The conventional mortgage is the most widely used, because it is the most readily available. In general, you must pay a higher down payment and more interest on conventional loans, and the repayment period is usually shorter.

Since in all cases—except the rare VA direct mortgage—you must apply to the lender for financing, this is where the shopping comes in. Try commercial banks, mutual savings banks, and savings and loan associations. At each institution, check the maximum mortgage available, the interest rates, the mortgage service fees, and any special features. Such features might be a prepayment clause—which enables you to pay off the rest of your mortgage without penalty if you strike it rich or decide to sell—or an open-end clause—which allows you to borrow on your mortgage at the original rate of interest.

If you buy a new house in a development, don't accept the developer's financing until you have checked other sources as well.

When you have a mortgage commitment from a lender, you and the seller will draw up a sales contract. Again you should call in your lawyer, for this is an important document. It specifies such items as improvements to be made by the seller, a legal description of the house, purchase price, date of occupation, and a list of any appliances or furnishings to be included in the deal.

Once the mortgage papers are signed, the property has been surveyed, and the title cleared, you are ready to close on the house. This transaction takes the form of a closing ceremony, at which you will finally get the mortgage papers into your own hands. But this comes only after you have endorsed the

Buying a New House?

To keep the house of your dreams from turning into a nightmare, you'll do well to give a new house the most critical going over. Here are some important facts to take into consideration.

THINGS YOU CAN'T SEE

▶ How thick are the interior walls? Wallboard must be ½ inch thick if rooms are to be quiet.

▶ Does the foundation have a poured concrete footing, and is it below the frost line? Check the builder's specifications to find out, because only this kind of foundation can prevent settling.

▶ Is the insulation thick enough? Don't settle for less than 3½ inches of thickness.

HEATING AND PLUMBING

▶ Does the house have a warm-air heating system? See if it has a 10-year guarantee on the heater, and a pully-driven air blower. Is it a hot-water system? The boiler should be guaranteed for at least 20 years. Look for the seals of the Institute of Boiler and Radiator Manufacturers, marked "IBR", and the American Society of Mechanical Engineers, marked "H". Is the heating gas? Check for the "AGA" seal of the American Gas Association.

▶ Are the hot-water pipes made of copper? Cold-water pipes can be of copper or plastic.

▶ What is the capacity of the hot-water heater? An electric one should hold 80 gallons, a gas one 40 to 50 gallons.

▶ How many electric circuits are in the electricity switchboard? A small house should have at least 8, a large one at least 12.

BATHROOM, WINDOWS, AND DOORS

▶ Is the toilet bowl of good quality? Test by flushing. If the water runs straight down the sides, it is very likely a cheaper model. If it runs down in separate streams, it is of a better quality. If the streams swirl, it is of a high grade.

▶ Do the fixtures have a trademark? This is a sign of first-line products. Are the faucet handles shaped like four spokes? This shows low quality.

▶ Do the outside doors shake if you rattle them by the knobs?

▶ Are the window sashes made of metal? If so, there should be plastic slide tracks for easier opening and shutting.

▶ Do window and door frames fit into the wall without gaps or cracks?

Comparing Home Loans

	Conventional	FHA*	VA
Amount you can borrow	Up to 90%—usually 75%—of property value, depending on the lender's policy.	Up to 97% of the first $15,000 appraised value; 90% on value over $15,000 up to $25,000; 80% on value over $25,000. Not over $33,000 can be insured.	Up to 100% of appraised value with a 60% guarantee on homes under $12,500 and a maximum guarantee of $7,500.
Size of down payment	Difference between amount borrowed and purchase price—usually 25%.	From 3% to 9% depending on property value, type of property and kind of loan.	No down payment required by VA—but lender may ask for a 10% down payment.
Time for repayment	Usually 20 years but may run up to 30 years.	Up to 30 or 35 years.	Up to 30 years.
Rate of interest (as of Oct. 1967)	6½% to 8% depending on lender, down payment time for repayment and local market conditions.	7% plus ½% for FHA insurance.	7%.
Special features and characteristics	Flexible. Requires 3 days to one week for approval. Typically requires larger down payment, shorter repayment than FHA or VA loans. Can sometimes be combined with second mortgage. Prepayment usually permitted with restrictions.	Insured by FHA to protect lenders. Regulated by FHA. Available with small down payment and long repayment period. Permits prepayment without penalty up to 15% in any one year. Includes FHA property appraisal. Usually requires 5 to 10 days for approval.	Available only to qualified veterans. Guaranteed by VA to protect lenders. Permits prepayment without penalty. Regulated by VA. Requires four to six weeks for approval. Available with lowest down payment, low rates, long repayment period.

*The FHA insures loans to veterans with more liberal terms. Subject to $200 cash outlay, veterans can borrow 100% up to $15,000 of appraised value; 90% of value over $15,000 up to $25,000; 85% of value over $25,000.

Source: "Your Housing Dollar"
Money Management Institute
Household Finance Corporation
Chicago, Illinois

Left: few people are lucky enough to have all of the three main types of home mortgages available to them, but a careful comparison of the sources that are open can help you get the best possible deal. This chart shows the difference in the cost of conventional, FHA, and VA loans.

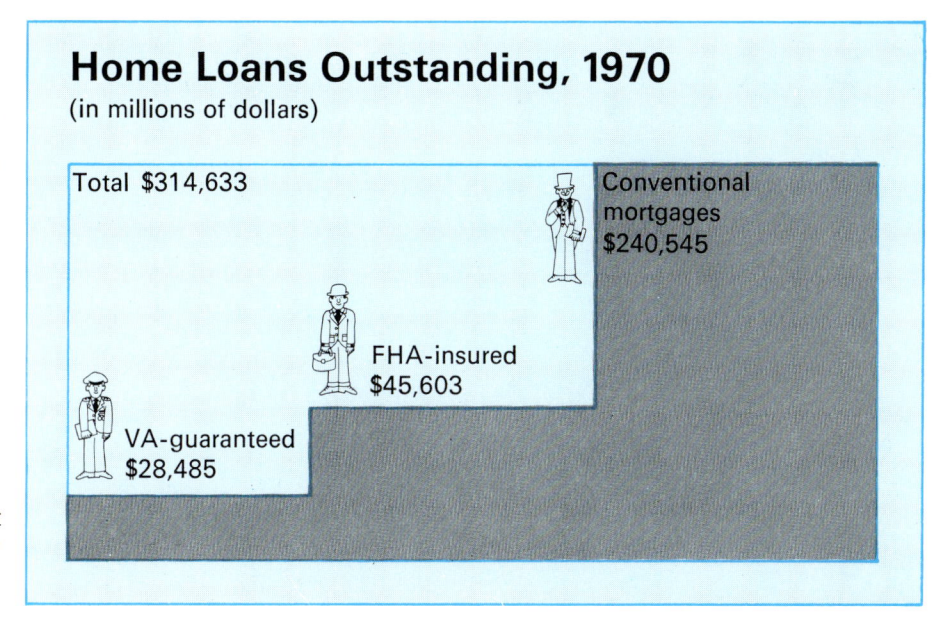

Right: it's clear from government statistics that most families must rely on conventional mortgages to buy their own home.

Home Loans Outstanding, 1970
(in millions of dollars)

Total $314,633
Conventional mortgages $240,545
FHA-insured $45,603
VA-guaranteed $28,485

check you got from the lender over to the seller of the house, and have committed the house as security for the loan. In addition, you will have to pay a grab-bag of fees known as closing costs. These can be unexpectedly high, but if your real estate lawyer has been earning his keep, you should have a good idea of how much you'll have to pay. It could be anything from $100 to over $1000. What for? For such things as mortgage service, property survey, title research and title insurance, and legal fees (beyond those for your own lawyer), and reimbursements for any prepayments the owner may have made for taxes, insurance, or fuel bills. With all these details out of the way, you can finally relax. The house is yours.

Remodeling
One of the biggest attractions of home-owning is the ability to remodel when and as you please. Say you have decided to redo the kitchen completely, or to add two rooms on the back. These kinds of big jobs mean a loan—and you should, of course, comparison shop for the best terms available.

Often the cheapest loan is an FHA Title I loan, which has an upper limit of about $5000. Aside from the low cost, there is protection and convenience when you do business with the FHA. Your signature is usually all the security needed to get the loan—provided your credit rating is good, of course. If a dealer or contractor arranges the loan for you, you can take comfort that he is probably reputable, since the FHA requires that he be approved by the lender. However, you can scratch the FHA as a likely source if you plan to build something luxurious, such as a swimming pool. Another alternative is to borrow on your mortgage, and, if you so wisely insisted on that open-end clause, it should be relatively easy. If money is tight though, or if you've only paid off a little of your mortgage, you may be refused this loan. You can then consider refinancing your mortgage by trying to get a new and larger one, big enough to cover your repayments and remodeling costs—but this can be expensive in the long run.

If the alterations on your house will take only a few hundred dollars, shop the banks for a personal loan, or a conventional home improvement loan. Either will probably be preferable to a loan from a finance company, which will run two to three times higher than the conventional bank rate.

The lure of saving money by do-it-yourself efforts is sometimes a trap. There is a double danger that materials will cost much more than you think, and that mistakes will have to be corrected at great cost. It may be cheaper, as well as easier, to get professionals on the job. If you do, be sure to get a contract that stipulates when the work is to be completed, and exactly what brands of materials are to be used. This is your best assurance of quick service and top quality.

Selling Your House
For the immediate future, the high demand for housing is expected to continue. Unless you've saddled yourself with a lemon, selling your home shouldn't be hard. If you do happen to hit a period of tight money, when high interest rates and hard-to-get mortgages discourage buyers, you have little choice but to wait it out.

Your first big concern will doubtless be your asking price. You can get clues from the prices in newspaper ads for comparable homes in your area. A good realtor can also be a great help because he will know the current state of the housing market. Having a realty agent handle the sale is a convenience on many counts. One of them is that he can show prospective buyers around if you are away from home during the day. You will have to pay the agent's fee, which is usually 6 per cent of the sale price, but you can come out even by including it in the asking price. Some agents like to have an exclusive on a house, which means that no other realtor can be involved. If you are anxious to sell, however, it may be smarter to get a multiple, or open, listing. This allows all the realtors in the listing group to have a go at finding a buyer.

If you are handling the sale yourself, you will have to depend largely on newspaper advertising for leads. Don't confine your ads to the local papers. Place them in surrounding towns, and nearby big cities, to try to cover commuters.

To make that important good first impression on prospective buyers, you will see that your house is in top condition for its age. Too much redecorating can boomerang, though. For example, Pat and Linda Nicholson thought they could get a better price if they did a massive sprucing up job. They put pine paneling in the cool, darkish basement to make it look warmer. They fitted a butcher-block table in one corner of the kitchen, and a built-in eating nook in another. They changed the chandelier in the living room for indirect, area lighting. All these changes made the house look a dream to them.

One of the greatest pleasures in owning your home is the chance you have to make improvements and additions as you choose and as your family needs them. Sometimes you can do the work yourself, as the woman above; but when it comes to a swimming pool, it takes a professional—and a lot of money. If you have to borrow to pay for improvements, be sure to shop around for the best credit terms.

Although the children's room was in obvious need of a major overhaul, the Nicholsons were emotionally and financially wrung by then. So they got an estimate of remodeling costs to show house hunters, and reduced the selling price accordingly.

What a shock awaited the Nicholsons! One otherwise delighted looker turned the house down because she wanted a cool, dark basement for a wine cellar. Others were put off by the kitchen built-ins, or the lack of a central lighting fixture in the main room. As the weeks dragged by, Pat and Linda realized that most people who are buying an older house prefer to redecorate to their own taste. Reducing the house price by the amount needed to redo the worst room had proved to be their best selling point.

Another must in selling your home is to learn which appliances are customarily part of the deal in your area. Usually the stove is included, but not the refrigerator. If there are other furnishings and equipment you want to sell, try to produce the original bills of purchase as evidence of when you bought them and how much you paid. On items such as drapes, carpets, and the like, consider yourself lucky if you get 25 per cent of what you paid.

Before you let a buyer assume your mortgage, get legal advice to be certain you are relieved of all responsibility if he defaults on his repayments.

Two final important warnings:

First, save all bills and records of expenses connected with buying and improving your home. Proof of this kind of expenditure can save you hundreds of tax dollars. Here's why. If you sell your house at more than its original cost, which gives you a profit, and then decide to buy a less expensive home, you'll have to pay tax on the profit. However, you'll get a tax reduction if you can prove that you spent money on home improvements.

Above all: don't impulsively accept the first buyer who comes along, or, conversely, don't refuse so many offers that you end up taking any price just to be done with it.

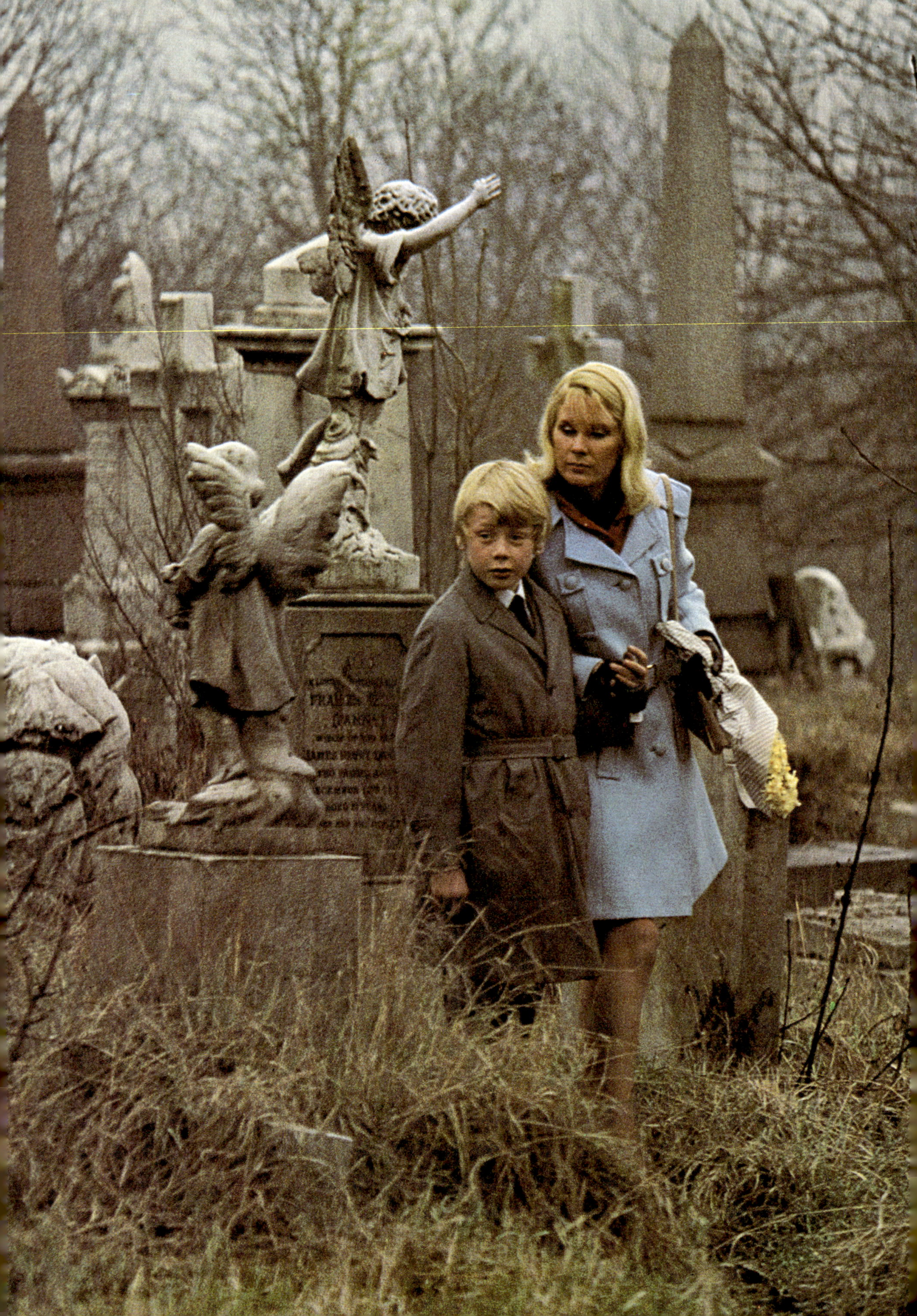

Buying Life and Health Insurance
6

The idea of being a young widow with children to raise is a grim one for any wife: the main purpose of life insurance is to eliminate worry about money from the unavoidable heartache of a family when the husband dies.

Frances Atkinson's father, Sam Barlow, died suddenly at the age of 56, leaving her mother widowed at age 50. In the shock of their grief, the family was further shocked to learn that there was a life insurance policy of only $7500. Frances, with a young family of her own, was worried about her mother's welfare. It was clear that Mrs. Barlow would have to find a job to support herself and the two teenagers still at home.

Things looked better after the estate was settled. Mr. Barlow proved to have been the careful provider Frances and the family thought him. Besides a savings account of about $10,000, Mr. Barlow had invested in stocks and bonds regularly on a small scale. These investments made up a supplementary income for Mrs. Barlow. The insurance benefits were enough for immediate cash needs connected with Mr. Barlow's death—the funeral and expenses of settling the estate—and for living costs for at least a few months. The house mortgage, too, was within months of being paid off.

Mrs. Barlow is not too badly off financially. She will probably have to work for some years to see the two children through school—though, of course, the savings account will help, as will the Social Security benefits due the boys from the federal government until they finish college. By then, she will be near the age for collecting full widow's Social Security benefits (62), and may have built up some job pension benefits of her own. In any case, the home will be hers free and clear, and she will have some income from the stocks and bonds.

This example shows how a family head can plan for his family's future security, using life insurance as *part* of the plan. It points up that insurance should not be looked at as an all-in-one savings, emergency, and retirement program. Had Mr. Barlow saddled himself with very high premium payments to buy massive amounts of insurance, he could not have made the other provisions for his wife. Moreover, with the constant inflation of present-day economies, he would have been paying for his insurance with money that was worth much more than the money Mrs. Barlow would later collect.

The story also points up another important fact about insurance: needs change as the family situation changes. Financial counselors say over and over that the young family with growing children needs insurance the most. A middle-aged widow with nearly grown children, like Mrs. Barlow, usually has other resources, and reduced needs in general. The elderly widow will need steady income more than the immediate cash benefits of insurance.

How, then, do you approach the extremely complicated subject of life insurance? This chapter, it is hoped, will point the way by giving you useful basic information on which to build your knowledge and understanding. Two main principles should soon become clear. One is that you should buy insurance to fit your needs, just as you do a house, a car, or furniture. The other is that you can save money by careful comparison shopping for whichever policies you decide on. To help you further, you will find much good material in the books listed at the end of this book. Remember, the better informed you are about life insurance, the wiser will be your buying decision.

To make a start, both wife and husband should understand a little about the kinds of insurance, and how they work.

The Two Types of Life Insurance
There are only two types of life insurance: *ordinary* and *term*. You will hear about wholelife, straight life, or cash-value insurance, but they are simply other *names* for ordinary life. You will also hear about

A father wants to make sure that his little daughter will never want for anything, even if he himself is not there to take care of her. But although insurance is based on this very emotional need, it is important to be as down-to-earth and critical about various policies available as about a new refrigerator. If under-insuring can be tragic, overspending on insurance is as wasteful as any other overspending. It is well worth taking time to work out the best insurance for your own individual family needs.

Below: in considering costs of insurance for adequate protection, a comparison between how much ordinary life and term policies will cost over the long run is helpful and necessary. As you can see, term insurance is considerably cheaper for many years.

endowment and retirement-income insurance, but they are simply other *forms* of ordinary life; they vary in that they come due after a fixed period, rather than on death.

By whatever name it is called, ordinary life provides basic insurance at the same time that it builds up a *cash reserve*. It stays in effect either until it is dropped by the policyholder, collected after a specified time (usually 20 years), or paid by the insurer on death of the policyholder. The cash reserve portion—commonly and inaccurately referred to as savings—can be borrowed against at relatively low interest rates.

Term insurance is basic life insurance alone, for a set period—usually five years. It must be renewed after each term, but renewal is generally guaranteed until age 65 or 70 without additional medical examinations to qualify. Premiums for term insurance are very cheap at the outset, but rise with each renewal at later ages.

You will find that insurance agents seem to resent the very existence of term insurance. They talk it down with arguments that it gives "temporary" protection, and

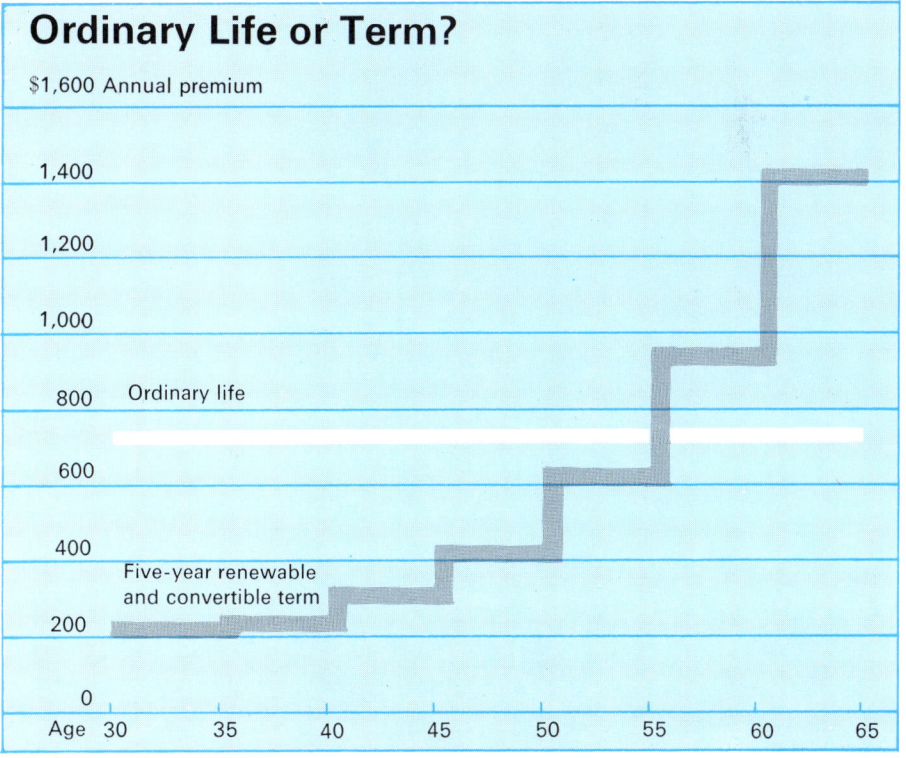

Ordinary Life or Term?

109

they talk ordinary life up with praise for the "forced savings" aspect of it. This one-sidedness of insurance salesmen makes it hard for you to get an absolutely clear understanding of their pet selling point of "forced savings". Let's take a hard look at it.

Bernard Parker had a $25,000 life insurance policy, and the last report from the insurer showed a $6250 cash reserve as part of that policy—that is, Bernard could at any time give up his policy, or cash it in, for a lump sum of $6250. His close friend Oscar Matthews had a term insurance of $25,000, and savings of $5,000 in a savings and loan association. It would seem, then, that Bernard was providing more for his wife in the event of his death than Oscar.

The two men died within a few months

of each other. The widowed Ruth Parker collected $25,000 in insurance benefits—and so did Sylvia Matthews. Now it was Sylvia who was the better provided for, since she had an extra $5000 in an outside account.

What happened to Bernard's cash-value insurance "savings"? The sad truth is, cash reserve doesn't exist as an extra sum to be paid on top of the face value of a policy.

Term Insurance

If you start buying a $25,000 5-year term policy at age 25 and keep renewing it until age 65 this is what you pay:

Age	Annual premium for each 5 year period
25	$104
30	106
35	119
40	155
45	213
50	302
55	431
60	665

Say you buy decreasing or reducing term insurance. In 10 years a $30,000 policy would decline thus:

Year	Face amount in force at the start of the year
1	$30,000
2	27,000
3	24,000
4	21,000
5	18,000
6	15,000
7	12,000
8	9,000
9	6,000
10	6,000

Source: Changing Times, March 1970

Left: perhaps the most important attribute of a well-worked-out insurance plan for a family would be flexibility, so that the coverage could be altered over the years. A couple in their 60's have usually outgrown much of the need for protection that was so vital in their 30's, when they had a growing family.

Above: term insurance is generally more flexible than ordinary life. The figures illustrate how you can keep your protection at the same level over the years by paying higher premiums at each renewal, or how you can allow the amount of protection to fall as your insurance needs decrease.

As the cash reserve grows year by year, the insurance protection is reduced accordingly. At the end, the so-called savings have, in a sense, swallowed up the insurance benefits to become the face value of the policy. In fact, the only way a policyholder can collect his cash reserve is to turn in his policy—so giving up his insurance protection in exchange. If he never touches his cash reserve—as in Bernard's case when his reserve had reached $6250—his beneficiary still will not get it *in addition* to the face value.

Another drawback of insurance-as-savings is that interest paid by insurance companies is among the lowest of any savings institution. Even the use of insurance savings as a quick and relatively low-cost source of loans won't stand up to careful analysis. First of all, the amount of protection is always reduced by the amount of the loan until it is repaid. If death comes before repayment, the beneficiary will not get even the full face value. Secondly, the policyholder must go on paying premiums while he is also repaying the loan, just as he would have to do if he had borrowed elsewhere.

Term Insurance Plus

Term insurance is unquestionably the simplest and cheapest life insurance. A young family head can buy $25,000 worth of term insurance for much less than he would have to pay for the same amount of ordinary life. Thus, he can afford more insurance protection during the critical years when his possible death might leave a young wife and small children without a breadwinner. With the difference saved in buying term insurance, the young family can make a start on its long-term savings program. For, as said before, life insurance alone is not enough.

Many insurance authorities today recommend that the best possible coverage for the young family is term insurance plus a regular program of savings. If the insurance agent's dire warning that "you say you will but you won't save" rings fearfully in your ears, enroll in your firm's payroll deduction plan for savings or investment in Government E Bonds. Most employers now do this. Your bank, too, will buy bonds regularly on your say-so. Or, even better, have your paycheck sent directly to the bank, and instruct the bank to transfer a set portion to a savings account every week. Whichever way you choose to save regularly, you will find your money grows faster than in an insurance policy.

Why You May Want Some of Both
Let's assume that you and your husband have had a long life together. You're both nearing 70. You've saved a good bit, invested a little, and are collecting the Social Security old-age payments coming to you. Things aren't bad, but you are still a bit worried about not having a single life insurance policy. The term insurance runs out in a few months, and you have discovered that renewal is almost impossible. If you can find an insurer willing to give you a policy at all, the price will be monumental.

This is where having kept a small ordinary life policy might have made you happier. Ordinary life insurance can be converted to *paid-up* or *extended* policies. In the first instance, the insured will get reduced coverage for the rest of his lifetime. In the second case, the beneficiary will be entitled to collect the full face value of the policy for a certain length of time after you complete payments, and further payments are not required for this added coverage.

Because of this convertible aspect of ordinary life insurance, financial experts often advise families to try to have some of both kinds of insurance.

Buying Insurance
There are numerous insurance companies, and they vary widely in what they charge and in what benefits they offer. To get the best value, you will have to compare many policies, both of different companies, and within one company. The clever insurance agent can always make the policy he is trying

Left: a good insurance agent can be a great help in planning a sensible insurance program for your family, but you can't leave the whole problem to him and expect to get the most economical policy best tailored to your needs. Like any major purchase (and any insurance policy costs a great deal over the years), wise buying of insurance requires that you do some homework. This means making many comparisons of companies and policies.

Right: be sure that you understand all the details in the contract. A good agent will be prepared to spend the time going through it with you, explaining wherever necessary. If he should try to rush you, get another agent.

to sell you seem to be exactly the right one for your needs, but beware of being overwhelmed. Don't make a decision without careful consideration, and a comprehensive investigation of the alternatives open to you. This is difficult advice to follow if the insurance agent calls on you, as often happens. When the agent is sitting across from you in your own home, there is a natural tendency to let social politeness get the better of your business sense. Added to that, insurance agents tend to be high-pressure, playing on your fears, and digging at your weaknesses. In your own home, with reminders all around you of just how important adequate insurance is, you will probably be particularly susceptible to this kind of scaremongering. Even if agents are low-pressure, they are generally extremely persuasive. So, steel your will, build up your powers of saying "no", and resist that sales talk. Remember, the agent is a good source of information if you insist on clear answers to your questions—and don't hesitate to ask as many questions as you must to make your understanding of this important matter greater.

Don't overlook the special insurance provisions you can get through a professional association. Teachers, lawyers, and other professions offer insurance coverage that can be worth your while. Usually these policies are some form of group term insurance. Their chief advantages are that their rates are low, and most do not require physical examinations in order to qualify for coverage.

The most reasonable way to buy insurance is through the bank, thereby avoiding the high cost of agents' commissions. However, this service is now available only in New York, Massachusetts, and Connecticut, where savings banks have been handling insurance since the early 1900's. Check the savings banks in your area. In your state they may be able to get you renewable term insurance cheaply through the Savings Bank Life Insurance Co. Keep in mind that the amount of insurance you can buy at banks is limited. For example, the top coverage available in Connecticut at this writing is $40,000.

It is impossible to summarize a topic as complicated and confusing—and as individual—as life insurance needs. Here are a few points to keep in mind, though.

It is the young family that needs insurance protection most, and that protection should be taken out on the head of the household only. Several small policies on other family members can leave you without sufficient money if the wage earner dies.

A regular process of savings and investments *plus* term insurance usually gives the best overall protection. As savings and investment earnings increase, the amount of insurance can, and should be, reduced.

In figuring insurance needs, take into account Social Security benefits. These include disability payment at any age, income in old age, and certain benefits to children in case of the father's death.

Remember that, in ordinary life coverage, a beneficiary gets only the face value of a

Whether you find yourself rushed to the hospital after an accident or chatting with your doctor after a routine checkup, you will find yourself with a hefty bill: medical treatment gets more and more expensive all the time. Medical insurance that gives adequate protection is an absolute necessity these days.

policy, and no extra amount of cash reserve.

Think of insurance as only part of your plans for future economic security. Don't overinsure, and so burden yourself with heavy premium payments for a long period of time.

Paying for Health Care

Everyone—single or married, young or old—needs protection in case of sickness or accident. In fact, it's financial suicide to be without health insurance today. Hospital charges are now pushing $100 *a day* in many big cities, and the cost of medicine has reached runaway proportions. The moderate income family justifiably fears being thrown into poverty in the face of a long or serious illness of any of its members.

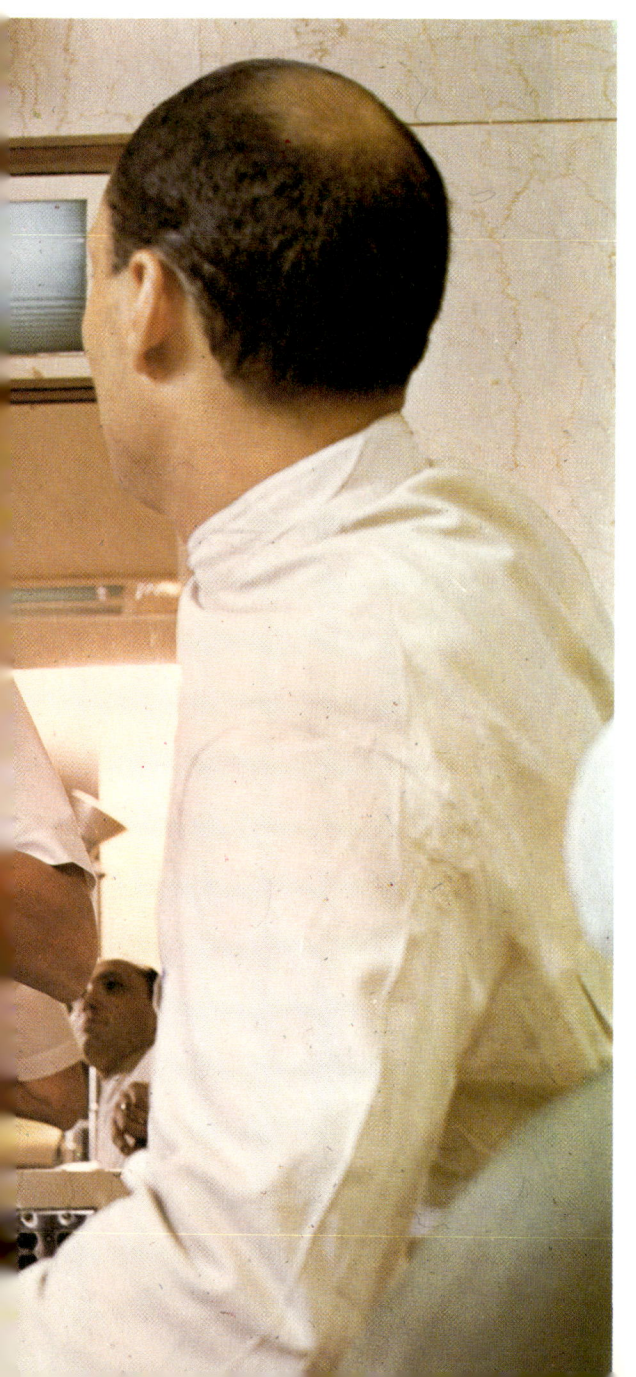

All health insurance policies have limits on how much of your medical bill they will pay, how long they will go on helping you pay, and what kind of care they will cover. That is why they are known as "basic health plans". That is also why it is vitally important for every family to set aside a cash reserve to be used exclusively for health emergencies. As a general guideline, you should have enough insurance to cover 75 to 80 per cent of hospital costs and doctors' fees, and plan to be able to handle the rest out of savings or current income if the illness is a minor one.

There are two main parts to basic health coverage, and it usually takes two policies to get them: hospitalization and medical-surgical protection. They go together like bread and butter. Hospitalization insurance pays for most of the expenses of a stay in the hospital for a certain period of time. Blue Cross is the familiar and widely available example of this type of coverage. Among the more common items covered under such a hospital plan are: bed and board, general nursing care, fees for the operating, delivery, or emergency room, X-rays and lab tests, drugs and medications, oxygen, anesthetics, bandages, and casts. Private rooms, telephones, and television are not included, nor are maternity services except in certain family plans. The other half of the basic coverage team is medical-surgical insurance. Blue Shield is the big name in this field. It covers the one important part of a hospital stay that the first policy did not—doctors' fees. Also included are surgical fees, services of an anesthetist, medical treatment, doctors' visits to your room, emergency medical care, in-hospital consultations with specialists, and shock therapy. Again, obstetrical services usually come only under a family contract. An unfortunate drawback of Blue Shield is that it varies greatly in different

Right: fortunately, not all trips to the hospital arise from calamities—but even the bills for the arrival of your new baby have to be paid. For young families, insurance to help with these "routine" medical expenses should be part of family planning.

areas of the country, and in some cases, gives very limited benefits.

There are some strictly local health insurance plans that give fairly comprehensive coverage, and you should investigate any in your region. These have the added advantage of providing preventive care because they pay for visits to the doctor on any medical matter, and include annual checkups. The Health Insurance Plan (HIP) of New York City, Group Health of Washington, D.C., Union Health Service Clinic of Chicago, and the San Diego Health Association are such local programs. They have their own doctors, their own medical centers, and sometimes their own hospitals.

Neither nationwide nor local plans offer dental care. Some union, company, and private association programs have added dental coverage in recent years; but, as a rule, you will have to search hard to find dental insurance.

Some private insurance companies offer what is called indemnity insurance for health protection. This pays a specified amount toward hospital room and board, and certain listed charges. If doctors' bills are covered at all, the insurance will pay only a given amount. This kind of insurance is somewhat costly as a supplementary plan, and not inclusive enough as a sole plan.

One other health insurance ought to be considered for families that can meet its high cost—and this means families in the upper income brackets. It is called Major-Medical insurance, and it is out-and-out expensive. Under Major-Medical, you pay the first $100, $250, or $500 of medical costs in or out of a hospital. The insurance then pays 75 to 80 per cent of the balance, which, depending on how much you pay in premiums, can be as high as $20,000. At this rate, Major-Medical insurance will help cover the huge bills that can quickly accumulate with a lengthy illness or serious injury.

Families of moderate income—from $8,000 to $10,000 a year—will generally do best with a combination of Blue Cross-Blue Shield, or with one of the local plans (HIP, Group Health) where available. The next best bet, though more costly, would be Blue Shield plus Major-Medical.

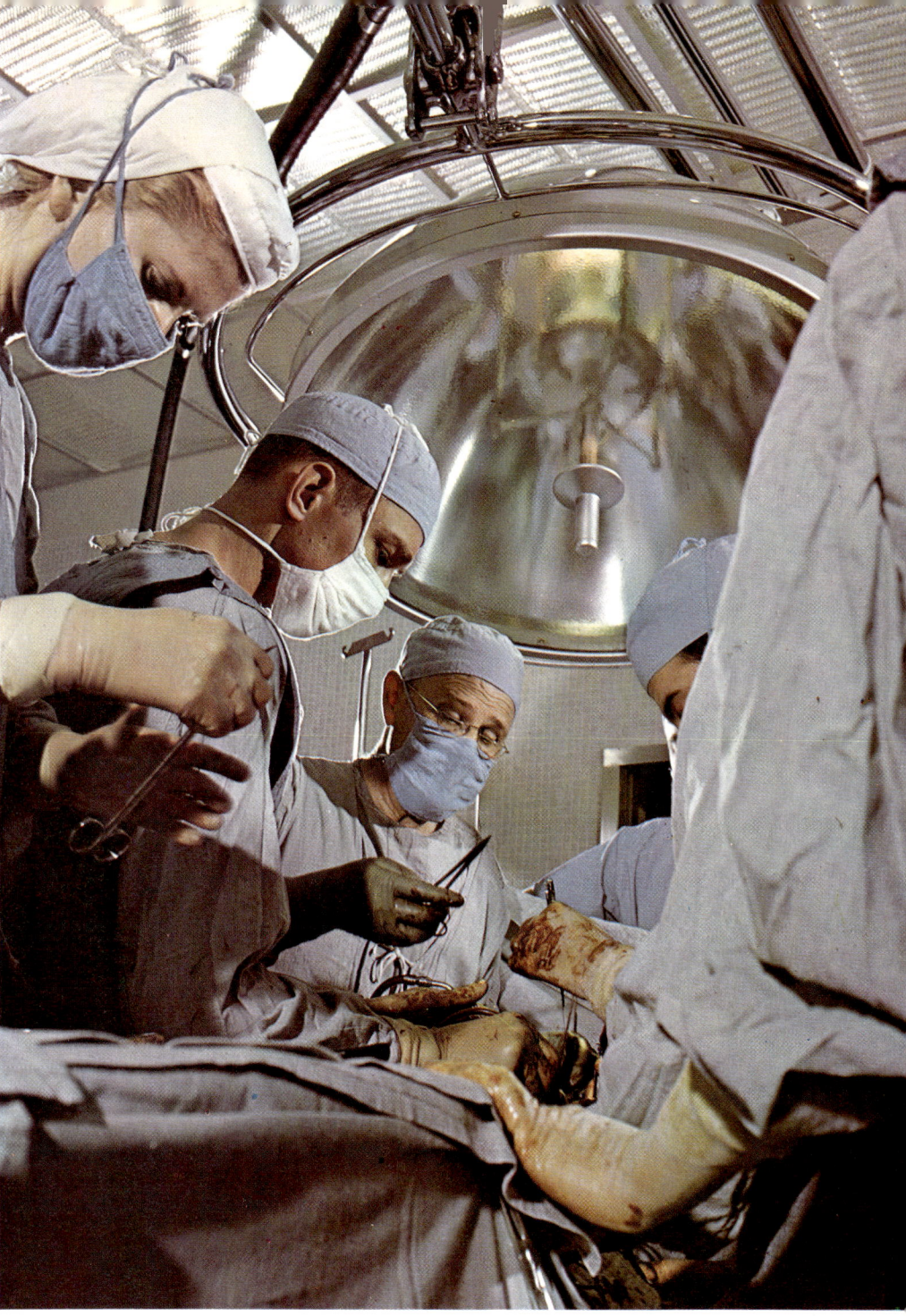

The most economical way to buy health insurance is through a group plan, which many companies of all sizes now make available to their employees. If you can't join a group plan where you work, you may be eligible through membership in a labor, cooperative, or professional organization. You might even get your own group together—it only takes three to qualify in

Above: surgical techniques become increasingly sophisticated, and costs go higher and higher. For families that can afford it, Major-Medical insurance will meet much of the cost of a very serious or prolonged illness or injury, in or out of the hospital.

117

Left: all drivers must have liability insurance, but if you have a new car, you will probably want comprehensive coverage to pay for damage in case you get into a collision.

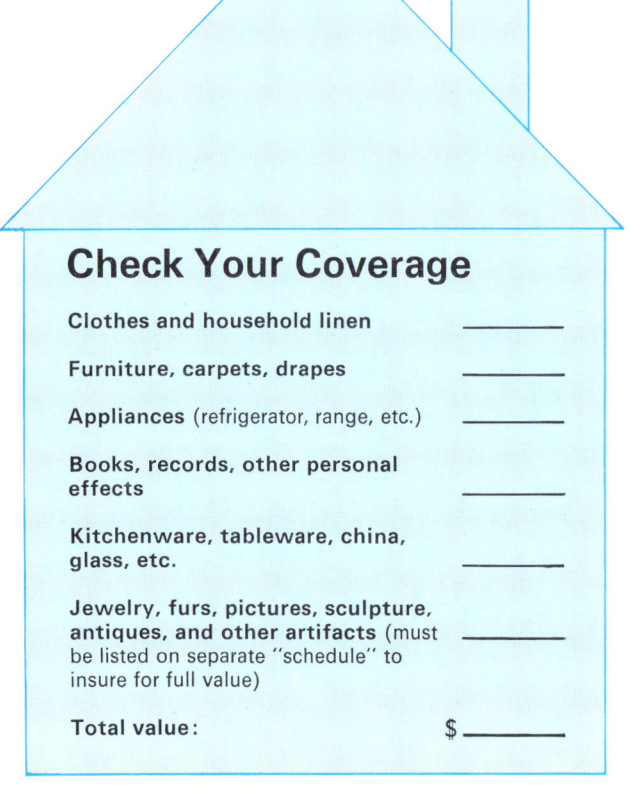

Right: the terror of a fire is something we all hope will never happen to us—but carrying fire insurance is only sensible. In figuring out how much insurance you really need, take into full account how much your house has increased in value, and how much it would cost to replace all your possessions.

Check Your Coverage

Clothes and household linen	_____
Furniture, carpets, drapes	_____
Appliances (refrigerator, range, etc.)	_____
Books, records, other personal effects	_____
Kitchenware, tableware, china, glass, etc.	_____
Jewelry, furs, pictures, sculpture, antiques, and other artifacts (must be listed on separate "schedule" to insure for full value)	_____
Total value:	$ _____

Left: here are some reminders of what to keep in mind when you are deciding how much homeowners insurance to buy. If you undervalue, you are sure to underinsure—and you'll be the loser in case of fire, theft, or property damage.

some areas, and ten will qualify just about everywhere. Group charges may be 20 to 40 per cent cheaper than an individual plan. This means that you might pay as little as $150 a year for a Blue Cross plan costing $250 a year for an individual family plan.

Here is a short checklist to help you measure up a health insurance policy. You should make comparisons whether you are buying an individual plan, or are part of a group insurance scheme.

Are hospital bed and board allowances high enough? A policy that pays only "up to $100 a week", as some do, is a drop in the bucket to what is needed for present hospital costs. Some policies pay room and board in full.

Are allowances for "ancillary", or "extra", hospital costs also high enough? Again, a plan that pays "up to $100" for such hospital charges as tests, drugs, bandages, and anesthetics, to name a few, is less desirable. Charges for extras can often equal the cost of room and board. Some policies have no limit on how much will be paid for ancillary services.

Will it cost you more to have a common operation than a rare one? Some health insurance plans have low allowances for operations you are more likely to need, such as an appendectomy or removal of a cyst. You get less protection if the high allowances are for the somewhat rare operations.

Is your protection reduced by restrictions on renewal or coverage? Make sure that the health insurance you buy is guaranteed to be renewable, and that it cannot be cancelled for *lifetime*. Be careful, too, that the policy does not cut out all coverage for existing conditions, even though most policies set a limit on such coverage. Without some protection on this point, you might find yourself unable to collect for an operation that was anticipated at the time you bought the insurance.

The great need for family health protection at reasonable cost has brought an upsurge in cheap mail order insurance. Consumer counselors warn one and all to stay away from them. Two good reasons why: coverage is often so limited as to be worthless; if you should have to sue to collect, you will have to go to the state in which the mail order firm was licensed in order to do so.

What about other family and property protection? It's easy to see that you need auto insurance only when you buy a car, or that you must increase homeowners insurance if you move to a bigger, more expensive house. Neither is it hard to relate needs for fire, theft, or personal liability insurance to what you own and where you live. Remember, though, you'll want to look at your coverage periodically to see that it keeps pace with increasing value of things, or replacement costs—that sofa you paid $285 for last year might easily cost $50 more to replace in a couple of years.

The suggestions given in this chapter are meant to help you decide how to fit insurance into your plan for family security—and also how to help you get more value out of the life and health insurance you do buy. If you review the situation about every five years to avoid being overinsured or underinsured, you will have mastered another technique in managing your money better.

You Too Can Invest!
7

Not long ago, it was only the rich who talked about stocks, bonds, and investments. Starting in the 1940's, the picture began to change. Today, people of moderate income are among those making up a virtual army of small investors—and many of them never dreamed of having a personal link to Wall Street high finance.

Why should you even think about stocks and bonds as part of your plan for future family security? The main reason is that some investments provide a hedge against inflation. You've run across these words in Chapter 5, when home ownership was also described as a hedge against inflation. It's an important concept, and here is what it means to you.

If you had $1000 in the bank five years ago, and kept it there, you would now have $1314 under the most favorable interest terms possible today. The total amount of money you have is greater, of course—but, because of inflation, what these dollars can buy is just about what the $1000 could have bought five years ago. You haven't made any progress—and if inflation continues, your money may buy even less. When you protect yourself against such a reduction in the purchasing power of money, you are hedging against inflation. A house, and certain kinds of investments, can give you that protection because their value will probably increase so greatly that, in money terms, they would bring you a big enough return to buy the same as or more than you can buy with today's currency.

Suppose, for example, that you invest in 100 shares of common stock at $10 each today. You might buy wall-to-wall carpeting with that $1000 in terms of its purchasing power. In ten years' time, those shares may be worth $6000, and, if you sold them, you would make a $5000 profit. Even if inflation had continued to eat away at the purchasing power of money, your $5000 would buy at least as good carpeting as you could buy today—and perhaps even a chair or a sofa in addition.

Notice that it is only common stock that is said to protect against inflation. Before going farther, let's find out more exactly what investment means, and how common stock fits into it.

Investing is putting your money into something that might bring you a profitable return. In doing so, you are taking a clear risk because, instead of making a profit, you might lose everything. Taking the example above, for instance, the value of your shares might have dropped to $5 each, and you would have been in the hole. That is why money management experts always advise that you invest only money that is truly "extra"—anything left after meeting all daily needs for food, clothing, and shelter; after providing adequate insurance protection; and after building up an emergency cash reserve of savings or government bonds that would see you through about a six-month period of difficulty.

Perhaps the preceding chapters have helped you to put your financial affairs in such good order that you do have an extra

Women are moving into the professional world of stocks and bonds. Muriel Siebert is the first woman member of the New York Stock Exchange, as head of her own firm. She argues that small investments, carefully chosen, can be profitable in most cases.

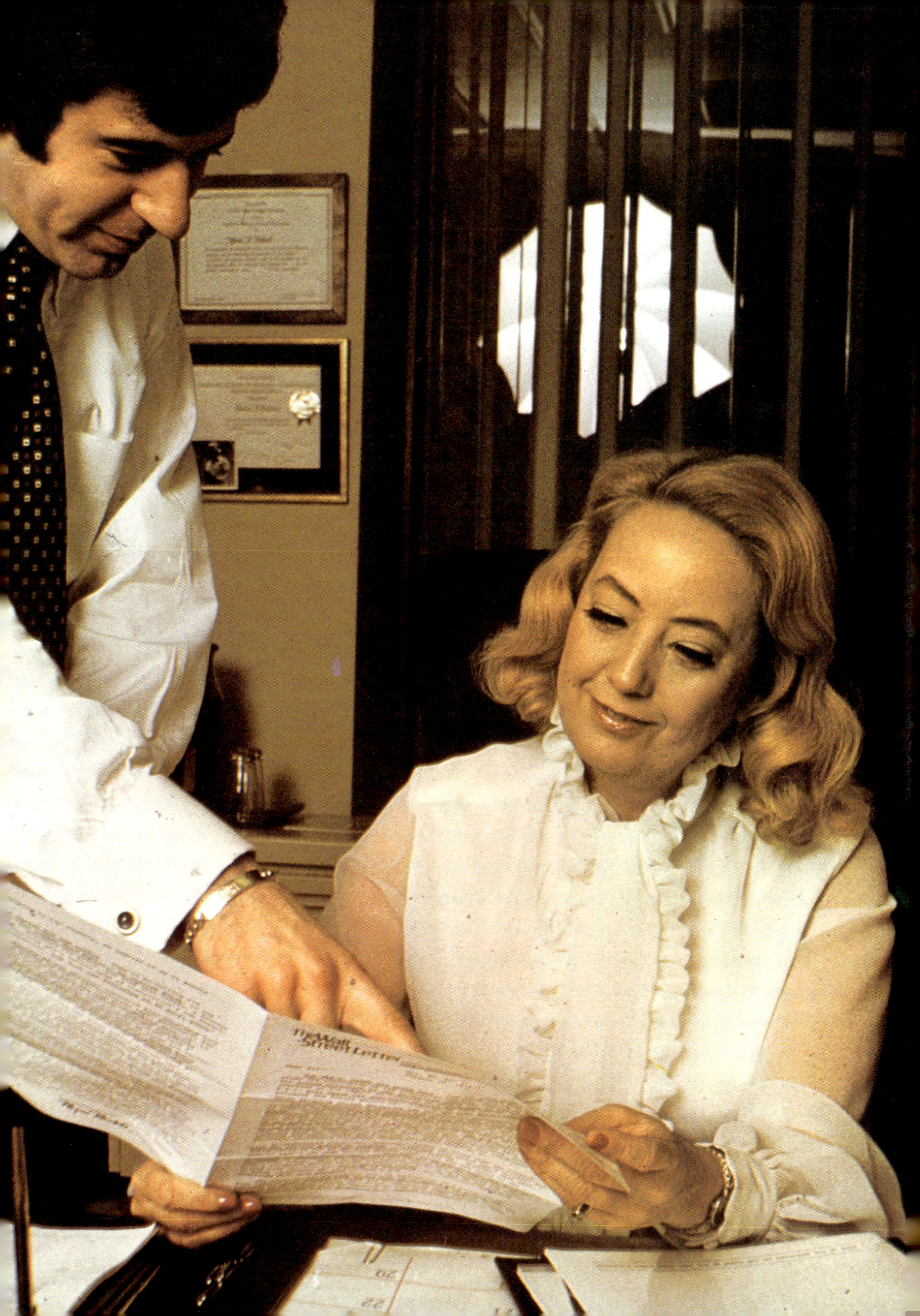

To outsiders, the New York Stock Exchange looks like a swarm of people milling back and forth at random. But in the midst of the apparent confusion, the brokers are buying and selling stocks and bonds of all American and foreign businesses listed on the famous Stock Exchange.

sum for investment every month. Then, and only then, you're ready to look seriously at putting your money into the nation's stock market.

The first thing you will find out is that there are different kinds of investments. Some can give you regular income, others may yield more money in total (capital gains), and still others might provide a combination of both. Your first decision, then, is what you want out of your investments—and this is often related to age.

People who start investing at an older age are likely to be more interested in getting steady income. They will probably want to invest in securities that pay regular dividends —bonds, preferred stock, or blue chip commons. Younger people can usually afford to wait for long-term growth when—if they are lucky and careful—the overall value of their investments should have increased greatly. They will probably choose common stock of the kind called "growth stocks".

What are these various securities?

The Kinds of Securities

A *bond* is like an I.O.U. on a loan you make to a company, which must pay you back in full later (usually after 20 years). Meantime the company pays a fixed rate of interest on the bond every year. A *stock* is a certificate of ownership in a company. As a stockholder, you share in a company's profits when it succeeds. *Preferred stock*, like a bond, pays a specified rate of return yearly. Both these securities are expensive, and few small investors can afford them. Besides, because their return is fixed, the earnings from them are always reduced in value by inflation, just like savings.

Common stock differs from preferred in that its dividends will vary according to how well the company does. However, if the business prospers, the value of the stock will go up whether or not the amount of dividends goes up as well. In fact, *growth stocks* rarely pay big dividends, and often pay none at all. This is because the companies that issue them—called growth companies

Following the Stock Market

As soon as you start investing, you will find it helpful—and necessary—to follow stock market information in the newspaper. Here is how stock market quotations are published in the special financial paper, the *Wall Street Journal.* It will give you an idea of what you have to learn in order to follow the day-by-day record of your stock. Remember, you'll have to follow the reports over a long period, and compare your stock regularly with several others in the same or related field, to measure how well it's doing. Note that the P-E Ratio is a good quick measure of investment value because it shows how other investors rate the stock. If your stock's P-E Ratio drops badly in comparison to others, it means that investors are losing confidence in its future success.

1	2	3	4	5	6	7	8	9	10
—1973— High	Low	Stocks	Div.	P-E Ratio	Sales 100s	High	Low	Close	Net Chg.
17⅞	14¼	PittFrg	.80b	11	15	14⅜	14⅜	14⅜	
47½	42	PittFtW	pf		z50	45	44	44	− 2¼
34⅞	24¼	Pittston	.60b	20	181	27⅛	26⅛	26⅝	− 1⅛
36 .	14¼	Pizza Hut		14	38	15¾	15¼	15¼	− ¼
7¼	3¼	Plan Resrch		12	18	3⅞	3¾	3¾	
19¼	11⅛	Playboy	.12	7	87	11½	10⅛	10⅛	− 1
2⅞	2⅜	Plessey	.10e	14	520	2¾	2⅝	2¾	+ ⅛
140⅜	103¼	Polaroid	.32	89	811	126	122	122½	− 4⅛
86¼	41⅞	Ponderosa	S	29	702	42⅜	40	41¼	− 1
20⅝	16⅛	PopeTa	.40b	5	37	19⅝	18⅞	18⅞	− ¾
18⅞	15⅛	Portecln	.80	7	2	15¼	15¼	15¼	....
22½	20⅜	PortGE	1.48	9	26	21	20⅞	20⅞	..
26	19½	PotlatchF	1	8	31	23	22½	22½	− ¼
16⅝	14⅝	PotmEl	1.08	9	99	15⅛	15	15	− ¼
54½	51	PotEl	pf4.04		z400	52½	52⅛	52½	+ ½
47	33⅜	PPGInd	1.50	7	137	34¼	33	33⅛	− ⅜
14⅝	8⅝	Premier	.30	10	1	9⅛	9⅛	9⅛	+ ⅛
18¼	13½	Premr	pf.90		1	13⅝	13⅝	13⅝	.
120	93	ProctG	1.56	27	237	99⅜	98½	99	− ⅞
9½	8¼	ProdRsh	.10	20	12	8½	8¼	. 8¼	
21⅞	14⅛	PSA Inc		11	84	15⅜	14½	14¾	+ ⅜
24⅛	18⅞	PSvCol	1.16	9	34	19⅞	19¾	19¾	− ¼
25¼	22⅞	PSvEG	1.72	9	95	23½	23¼	23½	.
122½	116	PSEG	pf9.62	.	z120	120	119¼	119½	+ ¼
107	101	PSEG	pf8.08	...	z340	105	104	104	
58½	55½	PSEG	pf4.30	...	z40	57	56½	57	+ ½

1 **High:** The highest price paid for the stock since the beginning of the year.

2 **Low:** The lowest price paid for the stock since the beginning of the year.

3 **Stocks:** The name of the company, generally in abbreviated form.

4 **Div:** The amount of the most recent quarterly dividend paid on each share.

5 **P-E Ratio:** This stands for price-earnings ratio. It is arrived at by dividing the price of the stock by its actual or indicated annual earnings per share. For example, if the price is $20 and the earnings per share are $2, the P-E ratio is 10. Using this example, the figure 10 means that buyers are willing to pay 10 times more for the stock than the current earnings of each share.

6 **Sales 100s:** Tells how many round lots of 100 shares were sold that day. Lots of less than 100 are not included.

7 **High:** The highest price paid for the stock that day.

8 **Low:** The lowest price paid for the stock that day.

9 **Close:** The last price paid for the stock at the close of business that day.

10 **Net Chg:** This stands for net change. It shows the difference between the last price paid for the stock that day and the closing price on the day before.

Mutual Funds

	1	3	4	5
		NAV	Offer Price	NAV Chg.
	Admiralty Funds:			
	Growth	4.48	4.91	− .10
	Income	3.93	4.31	− .01
	Insuran	8.46	9.27	− .13
	Adviser Fd	4.28	4.68	− .02
	Aetna Fnd	8.44	9.22	− .19
2	Afutur (v)	9.64	9.64	− .33
	AGE Fund	4.97	5.07	− .09
	Allstate	12.33	13.26	− .38
	Alpha Fnd	13.35	14.59	− .25
	Amcap Fd	5.13	5.61	− .24
	AmDiv Inv	9.90	10.82	− .15
	Am Equity	(z)	(z)	(z)

1 Name of Fund.

2 Securities invested in by the fund, by name or type.

3 **NAV:** This stands for *net asset value* per share. It is figured by valuing the total securities owned by the fund at the closing price that day, adding in the cash holdings of the fund that day, and dividing by the number of shares outstanding.

4 **Offer Price:** This is the cost of a share to the new investor; it includes the NAV plus the maximum sales charge in the case of load funds.

5 **NAV Chg:** The difference between the net asset value per share the day before and the day listed.

because of their rapid expansion—plow most of their profits back into the business so that *future earnings* will be greater.

Only when stock value goes up at a faster rate than inflation do you get a hedge against inflation through investment. Only risk investment in growth stocks has the possibility of giving you this hedge.

The stock of famous-name companies that have long made great profits and paid dividends steadily are known as *blue chips*. They are one of the safest forms of equity investment, but they are also high in price, and moderate in rate of return. Seldom are they recommended to the small investor.

You and Investing
Studying the stock market is time-consuming and difficult, but study it you must if you are to be an investor rather than a gambler. Your newspaper financial columns are the handiest source of information. In addition, you can get leaflets from brokerage firms, books from the library, and popular paperbacks on investing. Perhaps the best idea for beginners is to write to the New York Stock Exchange, Box 252, 11 Wall Street, New York, N.Y. 10005, and order the beginner's investing kit. It costs $1.50.

Another good idea for beginners is to make an experiment of investing for a period of about six months to a year, and decide only at the end of that time if investing fits into your family plan. You'll do even better to make part of the trial period—maybe three months—an absolutely dry run. That is, pick your stocks, follow their progress in the daily stock market reports, make decisions on buying or selling—but don't put a single penny into it. Wait until you get the hang of it before you consult a broker to place your first order. If you lose interest, get nervous, or find you just can't learn your way around during the experiment—give up. Peace of mind is worth a lot, too.

You and Your Broker
You must make many tricky judgments when you invest, and often the questions you have to answer stump even the experts. This is why you should always deal with a broker you can trust. You must order through a broker anyhow, and choosing the right one is as important as picking your family doctor. You should take the time and care to find the best one for you.

What is a broker and what does he do? A broker is a *registered representative* of a brokerage firm, and deals in buying and selling stocks on a full-time basis. Only if he is a member of the New York Stock Exchange can he place orders through that body. However, most brokerage firms either have one member who has a seat on the Exchange, or else they have an arrangement to deal through one or more Exchange members in other firms.

Time was when brokers wouldn't bother with the small investor, but most of them today will not turn you away. Not all brokers will act as advisers, and not all the advice they might give is necessarily good. But they can sometimes help the beginner learn the complicated operation—and the language—of the stock market, which is their business to know thoroughly.

When you look for a broker, visit three or four and compare how they treat you, and also what they tell you. A good test is to ask each of them about the same stock, so you can find out which one gives you the most information. If a broker asks you for a detailed financial history, don't be secretive and touchy. It's essential that he know everything about your money situation in order to give you sound advice. In fact, be worried if he doesn't ask all about you, just like a good doctor taking down your medical history. If he seems to want to get you out in a hurry, or if he doesn't give you his full attention, cross him off your list.

Try the biggest and best-known brokerage firm in your town, as well as others. It will cost you no more to deal with the best. Don't worry if your town is too small to provide you with a big choice. It may be an advantage in that the local broker will be so well known that you can check his reputation easily. If there is no reputable broker, write to the nearest city that has a New York Stock Exchange member firm. You can usually handle most of your business by mail. Above all, be sure to choose a broker whose firm is a member of the Security Investors Protective Corporation. This government-backed body insures you for up to $20,000 on your cash balance held by the brokerage, and up to $50,000 on cash and securities combined, in case the brokerage fails.

Be warned that once you give a broker the go-ahead, there is no turning back. You must be prepared to pay for any stocks you order within five business days. No broker will stand either for a change of mind about buying (though he will sell a stock again immediately if you really don't want it), or your failure to pay on time.

Remember, you always make the final decision, however much or little your broker discusses investment with you. You must learn all you can about the stock market yourself, follow it carefully, and take the responsibility for your success or failure.

You and Mutual Funds
Buying shares in mutual funds is one of the most popular ways for small investors to put professionals to work for them, and also to get a spread of various kinds of securities for greater safety in investing. *Mutual funds* are actually investment companies themselves. They pool the money of a group of small investors, and invest those pooled funds in a large number of companies.

Mutual funds grew like weeds after 1940, and numbered in the high hundreds by 1970. This means you are faced with a choice again—and it's like picking an individual stock when it comes to deciding which mutual fund best suits your purposes.

Like private investors, different kinds of mutual funds have different aims. Some try to assure you of a steady annual dividend as income. These are likely to invest mainly in bonds and preferred stock. Others seek to increase your capital greatly, and will probably concentrate on growth stocks. Still others aim to furnish both some regular income and some capital gains. They would tend to invest in all types of securities to achieve a balance.

Mutual funds are also divided into load and no-load types. *Load funds* charge a sizeable commission for their services, and have a widespread sales campaign. *No-load* funds charge nothing, and are harder to find. Don't assume, though, that you'll make more money in a no-load fund simply because there's no charge. This is not necessarily so.

When deciding on which mutual fund to buy, it's vital that you examine the past performance record of each one you might be interested in. Consult your broker and discuss it with him as fully as you would talk over one specific stock.

One more warning: be careful about *contract plans* for mutual funds. A contract looks attractive because it only costs $25 or so a month, and states that you can withdraw at any time after buying 9 per cent of the total you agree to. What it doesn't tell you, however, is that half the commission for the entire contract is taken out the first year. If you withdraw after a short time, you will have almost nothing to show for your investment.

Fortunately, other aspects of good money management are not as difficult to grasp as investing—and are basically more important in keeping you on an even keel financially. If you know more about planning a budget, day-to-day spending, credit, comparison shopping, insurance, and other topics covered in this book, you are well on the way to getting more out of your money. That means getting more out of life, too.

Right: money isn't everything in creating a happy family, but managing money well makes a big difference. Getting the most out of every dollar you have might allow something over for life's extras.

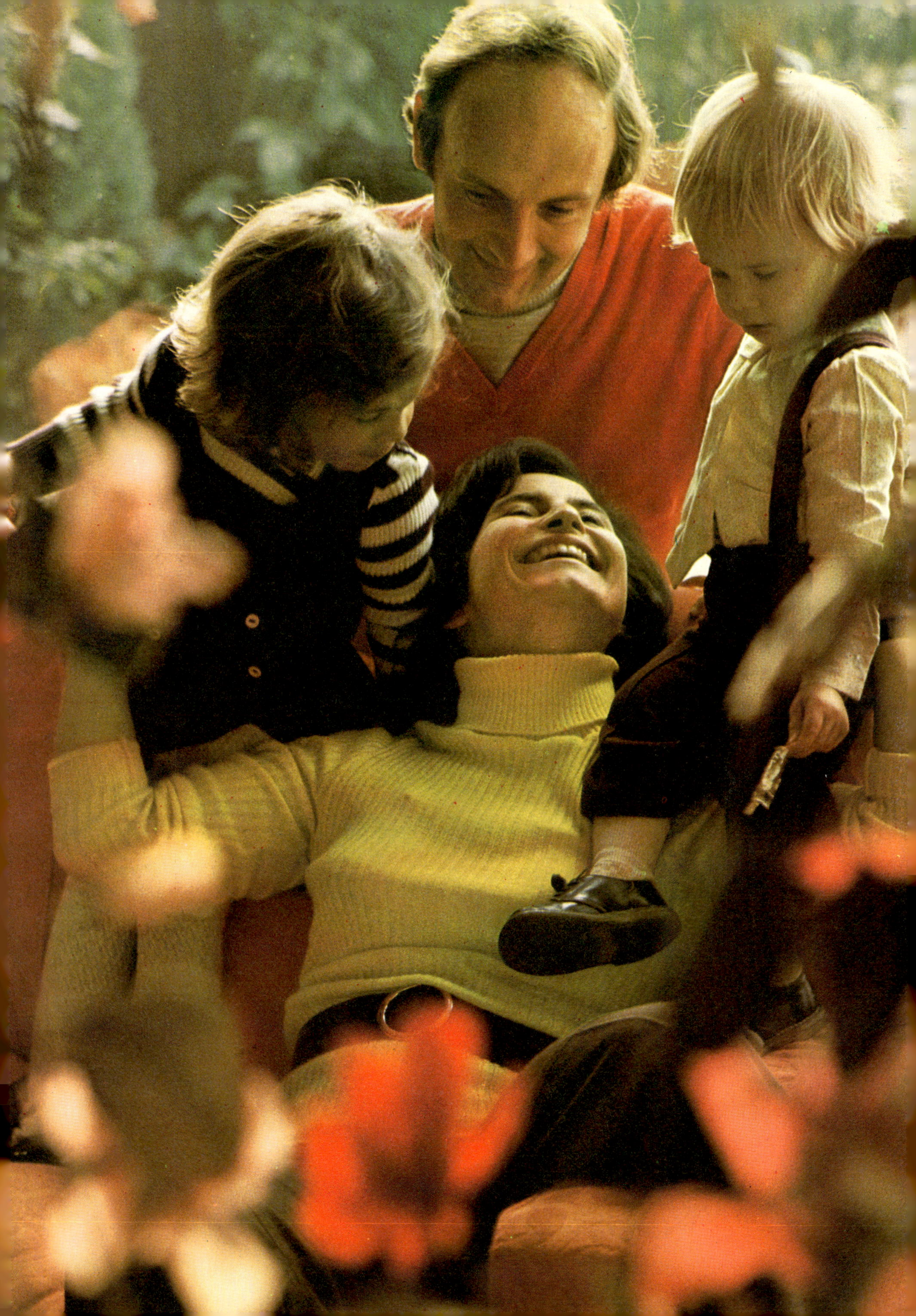

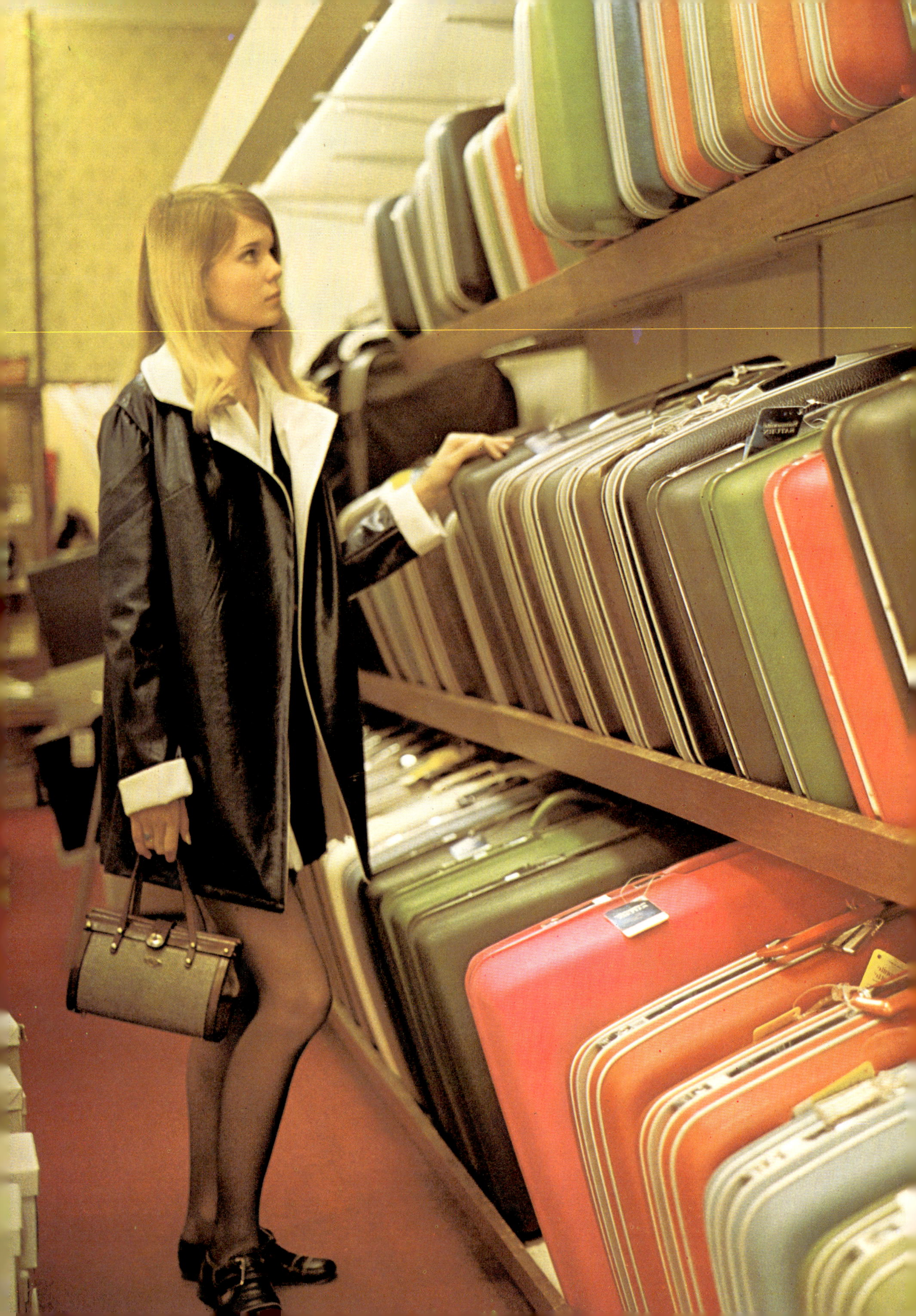

Questions & Answers

How can I best plan for my children's college education? How can I manage to buy the auto insurance I need as costs of this protection zoom? What can I learn about making better buys from clothing labels? Will Social Security really help me plan my retirement income? What do I need to know about home improvement and selling rackets in order not to be cheated?

The answers to these questions, and others like them, will give you important principles to go on in managing your money so that you can get more of the things you want out of life. Of course, no two people—and no two families—are alike. Therefore, some of the suggestions just won't suit you. The important thing, though, is to keep an open mind on what the experts say about wise spending and buying habits.

In the following pages, you will find information about college costs, scholarship aids, cheap student loans, and other sources of help in planning for your child's future education. On the topic of auto and homeowners insurance are tips on what kind of coverage to look for, and how to make savings in getting the coverage you need.

The answers to questions on labeling are intended to help you make better buys on clothing and household items. Then there are suggestions on how labels can help you make what you buy last longer.

The section on Social Security and Medicare will give you a good idea of what you can expect from the federal government's programs for the elderly. This should be useful not only to you yourself, but also to your parents or other elderly relatives.

Finally, you will find detailed information on a few of the rackets that yearly rob millions of Americans. With this information, you can arm yourself against being taken on some of the most common home improvement and general selling swindles.

No book can, or should, dictate the choices you make in allocating your money. The intention of this book, and these questions, is simply to help you base your choices on sounder economic knowledge.

Whether you are buying a new piece of luggage or family insurance protection, the daily groceries or a college education, it pays to put your mind and energy into getting your money's worth for what you spend. Whatever your income, life will be more pleasant and more rewarding if you bring some order and sense into your money management.

129

Education Planning

We would like to put our children through college, but before we start making plans for financing them, I'd like to know if their chances of a college education are good in this country.

Yes, statistics show that a great number of young Americans have—or make their own—opportunity to get a college education. In 1972, about 50 per cent of high school graduates went on for advanced study. According to education experts, that already high figure is expected to go up to 63.1 per cent by 1980.

This high college entry rate often represents great sacrifice on the part of parents. More and more parents, it seems, take it as a matter of course that their children *must* have a university education, and plan family goals in that light. However, some youngsters don't in the least want more schooling—and, perhaps, would be happier going directly to work, or taking a short technical or vocational course, right after high school. Shouldn't you think about the possibility of *not* sending your children to college? If, for example, your son is dead set on being a policeman, or your daughter wants only to be a forest ranger, then they don't need classes in mid-18th-century French literature. Don't force such youngsters to go to college—it will only make them miserable for four years of their lives. Of course, you must be as sure as you can that they are settled in their decision; but even if they have second thoughts later, all is not lost. Since the post-World War II years of heavy enrollment by mature veterans, it's a common sight to see older students enter college as freshmen.

What should I know about the probable cost of higher education?

Like housing, food, and just about everything else, the cost of higher education keeps shooting up. This is a fact you should hold firmly in mind when making future plans, especially if you have more than one child to educate. Right now, you can easily face an outlay of about $3200 a year in private colleges, and about $1500 even in publicly-supported institutions—and this covers only the main costs of tuition, fees, and room and board. Books, supplies, clothing, entertainment, travel to and from home, and still other expenses can about double these figures. You will do well to add a 5 per cent per year increase on present rates of an average college in estimating future education expenses.

We were planning to send our daughter to the state university, but we also have a junior college with a good scholastic rating near home. She could go there while still living with us. How should we make our choice?

You are lucky to have this kind of choice, and wise to consider both of these schools. Many parents forget that state and city colleges, supported by their own tax money, offer good educational facilities. In fact, some of the tax-supported institutions are superior, ranking among the finest in the land. Yet their tuition is generally reasonable for residents of the state or city in which they are located. A few of these colleges are even free.

Your own decision, of course, must depend both on your finances and on your daughter's personality and desires. If your child can, and will, stay at home while attending a nearby college, so much the better for your pocketbook. You will save all the costs of room and board, which are a big slice of the educational bill. You will also save on travel expenses.

As to your daughter's attitude, will she feel cheated of campus life if she stays home? Or can she be persuaded to postpone savoring her independence in order to reduce your financial problems? If the latter is true, she'll probably be delighted to go to the neighboring junior college.

Has she settled on a future job? Is it a vocation that doesn't require four years of college? A two-year school can provide an excellent education for the student who has chosen a vocation. At the same time, it can also be a stepping stone into a four-year college if his or her plans change.

Whatever decision you make, it will be a happier one if you can all talk it over and agree among you as a family.

What about scholarships?
If your son or daughter is an exceptional student, he or she might have a chance to win one of the well-known National Merit Scholarships. There are 2000 of these given each year, but there is also strong competition for them. Students must take a tough three-hour test, and make a high score on it, to qualify for these scholarships at all. Awards vary in dollar amounts, depending on the financial needs of the winners. The highest National Merit Scholarship is $1500 per year. There are also special National Merit Scholarships for black students.

The qualifying tests for National Merit Scholarships are given through the nation's high schools, and practically all high schools in the country participate in the program. Tests usually fall in February, but exact information can be obtained from the local high school's principle or guidance counselor.

There are also numerous small scholarships around, some as little as $25 or $50 a year (but every little bit helps). The average award is about $550 a year.

Many students help themselves along by working part time while in school, and full time during the long summer recess. A wide variety of part-time jobs exist on any college campus—typing, working in the library, or waiting on tables, for example. These jobs are not particularly well paid, but they are a source of spending money, at least. Full-time summer jobs, although sometimes hard to find, can bring in considerable earnings.

Once in school, students can make a savings by buying secondhand textbooks, and reselling them after the courses are finished. Most colleges have bookstores that sell and buy back the standard texts.

In all honesty, I don't trust myself never to touch any savings I start for my youngster's college education. Isn't an endowment policy the answer for someone like me?
Frankly, endowment policies are hardly the answer for anyone. The big sell will have you believe that they are great for education planning (it's that "forced savings" sales talk again), but be wary. Remember that an endowment is simply an ordinary life insurance policy that you pay off in a fixed period, usually 15 or 20 years. Even if you start a 20-year endowment when the first squall comes from the cradle, you won't have cash-in-hand at the start of college. It's an expensive way to save, too, because interest rates are among the lowest there are, and premiums are comparatively high. Endowment policies also give scanty life insurance protection.

If you still resort to insurance "forced savings", it makes sense to add an "endorsement" to your policy for a small additional charge. Then, if you die or become too disabled to work, the cash value won't be lost. You won't have to pay any more premiums, but your beneficiary will still collect when the policy comes due.

My teenager's college fund went down with most of our rainy-day savings to keep my father in a decent nursing home his last three years. Now I have to borrow for college expenses. How should I shop for the cheapest loan?
Students themselves get the best break on education loans, so it might be best for your son, or daughter, to be the borrower. (You could always help on repayment when your situation eases.) The least expensive loan is available from the federal government, under the National Defense Education Act of 1958. The next cheapest loan is made by states—though not all of them—through a guaranteed loan program.

The federal government will lend a full-time student up to $1000 per year, and up to $5000 over all the years of schooling, at an interest rate of 3 per cent. Repayment does not start until 9 months after the student finishes or leaves school, and can be spread over a 10-year period if desired. Those who become teachers get a further break. Their loan can be reduced by half if they stay in teaching for at least five years. In all cases, the debt is canceled if the borrower dies or becomes totally disabled before repaying.

For full details on National Defense loans, send for leaflet FS 5255:55 039, *Borrowing for College,* from Superintendent of Documents, Government Printing Office, Washington, D.C. 20402. There is a small charge.

Nearly 40 states have college loan programs, ranging from very good to merely token. The programs are operated through local commercial banks, which make all arrangements for loans at the going interest rate of 7 or 8 per cent. However, the student pays only 3 or 4 per cent interest, and the state pays the difference. Loans are given only to state residents, but the money can be used outside the state. Repayment begins from 9 to 12 months after graduation.

New York leads the states in providing a first-rate student loan program. Among other good ones are California, Illinois, Massachusetts, Michigan, New Jersey, Ohio, Rhode Island, and Virginia. To find out what your state offers, write to the State Education Department in your state capital.

Don't let your youngster give up if one bank turns him down for a loan. Encourage him to apply to a half dozen or more other banks. This kind of persistence can pay off.

About 75 per cent of the nation's colleges have loan programs, some of which go easy on repayment schedules. Other sources include labor unions, churches, and civic organizations such as the Kiwanis, Lions, and Rotary Clubs. These are too varied to describe here, and information is not usually difficult to get.

If all fails and you—the parents—have to borrow, you will have to shop around for the best deal, just as for a personal loan. Stay away from finance companies, which run such dignified-sounding outfits as Education Funds, Inc., and Tuition Plan, Inc. Their true interest rates can reach 55 per cent.

As the day of college entry gets nearer, where can I get practical help in planning college finances?
The guidance counselor in the local junior high or high school is a golden source of information. Consult her as soon as your youngster is in 8th or 9th grade, and she can help you get a head start on practical planning. Guidance counselors know which schools cost what as to tuition and living expenses, and also know about the many little things that add up to a lot—such as snack foods, laundry, on-campus travel, dues for fraternities or clubs, and entertainment. These are costs you have to estimate in making a sensible budget.

Guidance counselors also know the best sources for loans and scholarships, and how to apply for them. In addition, they are familiar with part-time work opportunities, and can give a good idea of the earnings that can be expected during the academic year.

If you already know which college your son or daughter is going to, you can consult the financial aid officer at that school for specific information on loans, scholarships, and part-time jobs. The financial officer will also be able to give guidance on miscellaneous expenses.

Auto Insurance

I know that I can't drive legally without being insured, but auto insurance is a great expense. How can I save on it?
There are some companies that sell auto insurance more cheaply, and some policies that offer "special treatment" savings. You will simply have to shop widely to get the best possible rates for the coverage you need.

One source you might try is an insurance broker—but be sure to talk to two or three before you decide anything. Brokers not only know many different companies and policies well, but can also advise you on which kind of coverage gives you the most.

Another way of getting auto insurance at more reasonable prices is to deal with companies that don't sell through agents. (You save on the big commissions agents get.)

Looking into policies that give special treatment to certain drivers is still another way to save. Among those who can often get reduced rates on insurance are drivers with good safety records, young people who have taken driver training courses in high school or college, and students with high grades.

To qualify for a safe driver policy, you must have, and keep, a near-perfect driving record. Your record is checked every 3 to 5 years—and this may cause problems for you. It has been found that rates can go up drastically under a safe driver policy as soon as you have an accident—even a minor one. Minor traffic convictions, too, can cause rates to shoot up out of all proportion to the offense. Insurance experts caution you to be extremely careful about buying a safe driver policy. After all, even the best of drivers scratch fenders once in a while, or get a speeding ticket. If such small mistakes cost you a fortune in increased insurance rates, it's hardly worth it.

What kind of automobile insurance will give me and my family the most protection?

The one protection every driver should get as much of as possible is *liability* insurance. In fact, you must by law meet your state's minimum requirement, if it sets one; but you should have much more than any state minimum. Liability insurance actually protects others against you by paying for any injury you might do them to body or property—and court awards in accident cases resulting in serious disablement or death can wipe you out financially. There is simply no limit to the amount of money you might have to pay, so the more you can meet through your insurance, the better.

The amount of coverage in liability insurance is shown by three figures. For example, 10/25/5 means that the insurance company will pay $10,000 for one person killed or injured by you, $25,000 for all killed or injured by you in a single accident, and $5000 for damage to property, mainly the car that was hit. In case of a lawsuit, anything the court gives above these figures —and it can be astronomical—must be met by the insured. To skimp on liability coverage is to be worse than foolhardy. If you have to forego other insurance on your car, you should buy the greatest amount of liability you can. The cost of more coverage is fairly reasonable, because a small extra premium brings a large increase in protection. For example, if 10/25/5 costs $100 a year, another $15 a year gets 20/40/5, another $19 gets 25/50/5, and steps up in like proportion can get 300/500/10 with a $47 a year additional premium on the base. You should try to carry the last-named amount if possible.

Another important aspect of liability insurance is that one policy covers the car owner, other members of his family, anyone using the car with permission, and the owner and his wife when driving a car not their own. If you have teenagers or young adults under about age 25 using your car, the premium may go up somewhat, but the coverage is more vital than ever.

Can I do without collision and/or comprehensive insurance for my car?

You can certainly economize on collision and comprehensive insurance, even if you decide you can't do without them entirely. Collision insurance merely pays for repairs to your car in any kind of accident. Because benefits go down in accordance with a car's age you probably won't get enough money to matter if your car is more than 3 or 4 years old. Therefore, you can almost surely do without collision insurance on an old car. Looking at it from another angle, even a series of small repairs could cost you less than the amount of the insurance premium. Besides, insurance companies often penalize you for making small claims—even though you have every right to— by canceling your policy. This legal, if immoral, pressure on you to pay for your own repairs makes collision insurance practically useless for small claims.

If you feel it's too big a gamble to drive without collision insurance, especially if your car is new, you can still make savings by buying $50, $100, or $250 deductible coverage. This means you pay the first $50, $100, or $250 of any repair bill. Take the biggest deduction you can handle, because there is about $60 per year spread between the lowest and highest deductible.

Comprehensive auto insurance covers theft, fire, and damage or destruction of the car by causes other than collision, such as hurricane or flood. It is not an expensive coverage by and large, and can be further reduced in cost with a $50 deductible policy. However, you may have great difficulty in getting comprehensive insurance if you live in an area where car stealing is common.

I've heard about many other kinds of auto insurance. How can I tell which are important and necessary?
There are two other kinds of highly recommended auto insurance, and their cost is low enough to make you think twice about doing without them. One is *medical payments* insurance. This pays for medical treatment, hospitalization, and funerals of all occupants injured or killed in your car, up to the amount of coverage. Payment will be made no matter who was driving, or whether the accident was the driver's fault. You shouldn't be driving without at least $2000 of medical payments insurance, which will cost only a few dollars a year.

The other low-cost auto insurance you should carry is called *uninsured motorist* coverage. With this coverage, you will be able to collect damages if you are hurt by a driver who has no insurance to help him pay you. This protection will cost about $2 or $3 per year.

Homeowners Insurance

Is it true that a package policy is the cheapest and best way to get more insurance protection for the home? If so, what is covered?
Buying insurance in bits and pieces is an expensive way of buying protection. That is why package policies for homeowners have almost entirely replaced separate policies. The various packages themselves range from the most basic to the fullest possible coverage, and so vary in cost, of course. So you must still decide carefully what you need, in line with what you can afford.

The names and types of homeowners policies differ in different parts of the country, but they all cover both house and personal property. It might be easier to look at what almost all policies have in common before talking about variations.

An important part of any homeowners policy is protection for personal property. This means all that's in your house, both in the way of furnishings and personal effects. You will have to pay more to cover valuables, such as paintings, antiques, jewels, and furs, to their full value. (They are then "scheduled", or itemized, in an attached form.) You can also pay a little more to cover theft or damage of personal effects when in use away from home.

Most homeowners packages offer liability coverage. Like the liability part of auto insurance, this helps you pay others who might be injured or killed on your property, whether you are to blame or not. For example, an unknown child might wander all uninvited into your yard, and climb the sycamore tree for fun. If he falls and breaks a few bones, you might have to pay heavily. Your homeowners policy helps to pay, up to the standard limit of $25,000.

Did you ever stop to think how expensive it would be to live in a hotel and eat out if your house burned down? Most homeowners policies will help you meet living costs in such a case, up to the limit set in the policy.

Almost every package policy also has these additional features: medical payments, usually up to $500, for those injured in your house (from a fall down the stairs, for example); and payment for damage to the property of others—like when you accidentally knock down part of your neighbor's fence as you turn into your own driveway.

It is on protection for the house that package policies differ most, and they generally fall into three forms. The *basic form* covers only the most common dangers to your home. These include fire, lightning, windstorm, hail, vandalism, riots, and theft.

The *broad form* covers the most common, plus several other less common, dangers. These include building collapse, falling objects, weight of ice and snow, and certain accidents caused by heating systems and electrical equipment. The *comprehensive form* gives such complete coverage that it doesn't even try to list everything. Instead, it lists only what it doesn't cover—and these exceptions are full-scale disasters such as war, earthquakes, tidal waves, and landslides.

If you follow the advice of many insurance experts, you will get the broad form on house protection within your homeowners package. With it, you will be well guarded against the most probable dangers, and the cost will be moderate.

A friend of mine lost his home in a fire, and his insurance company only paid him part of what the house was worth. How can I guard against such a thing happening to me?
Probably your friend was underinsured. To avoid this situation, you must insure your house for at least 80 per cent of its full market value at the outset, and increase your insurance coverage as the value of your house increases. If you don't, your insurance company will only pay at a reduced rate in case your home is destroyed. You can easily slip into the position of being underinsured if you don't make a periodic review to be sure you have enough coverage.

What about insurance for people who rent?
There is also a package policy for tenants in apartments or houses. It is like the other homeowners policies as to theft, liability, medical payments, and other protection, and includes the broad form coverage on the contents of the rented premises. You must insure for at least $4000 to get this package.

Labeling

Can I wash my son's easy-care poplin jacket and my daughter's drip-dry permanently pleated skirt in the same machine load?
Most easy-care and drip-dry fabrics can be machine washed, but often there are special instructions as to water temperature, number of cycles, and drying. Your question was probably answered on labels telling exactly how to care for the two garments, but it's understandable if you lost or misplaced them. Now, a new law passed in July 1972 takes all the questions out of what kind of care will keep clothes in good condition, and make them last longer. From now on, garments must have easy-to-read care labels sewed into, or otherwise permanently attached, to them in an easy-to-find spot. If a poplin jacket should be turned inside out to wash, you'll see the directions that say so every time you wash it.

Checking the care label is important even if the garment should be dry cleaned. Sometimes, for example, it will advise you to tell the dry cleaner the exact fiber content.

If you do a lot of home sewing yourself, be sure to ask the yard goods salesperson to give you the right care label for whichever textiles you buy—and sew it into the finished clothes. After that, no more guesswork, and no more mistakes, on how to wash, bleach, dry, iron, or dry clean properly.

The cotton curtains in my very sunny den have faded hopelessly, and must be replaced. How can I avoid sun fading the next time?
Look for the label that says "vat dyed" to get the most colorfast fabrics. Colorfastness is especially important in curtains and drapes, and vat dyed material will usually withstand fairly strong and steady sunlight. (It will also keep its color through many washings or cleanings.) The "sunfast" label is the next best guarantee against fading caused by the sun. Finally, "sun resistant" material is a pretty good bet. This label means that there shouldn't be more than slight fading from strong light.

A label is only helpful if you know exactly what it means, but that meaning is not always clear. Here are a few useful label terms to keep in mind.

In regard to shrinkage, the "sanforized" label means that the fabric or garment will not shrink more than 1 per cent. If marked "preshrunk", the shrinkage might be as much as 3 per cent.

On special finish fabrics, one marked "water repellent" is treated to make the water roll off. After a cleaning or two, a water repellent garment might have to be retreated. This differs from waterproofing. A "waterproof" fabric is permanently coated with plastic or rubber. Water can't get through, but neither can air. That's why waterproofed material makes the wearer feel uncomfortably hot and sticky.

"Scotchgard" is another treatment of fabric that sheds fluids, and it also resists stains. It works by keeping stains floating on top so that they can be easily removed with a cloth. Scotchgard treatment makes care of carpets, sofas, and other materials subjected to especially heavy wear much easier.

Labels on sheets and pillowcases show "thread count". What does this mean?
The thread count tells you how many threads per inch were used in weaving the fabric for sheets and pillowcases. It's important to you because a high count means a strong weave, and a strong weave means greater durability.

The two most often used textiles for sheets are muslin and percale. Of these, the rougher textured muslin is cheaper. A thread count of 140-148 is high for muslin.

Medium thread count for percale is 186-190, and this will usually give good wear. You'll often find 186-count percale sheets at prices cheaper than muslin in white sales—and these will be one of your best buys. Look for 200-count percale in the January and August sales too. They are frequently bargain priced. Remember that 170 is low for percale; a high-count muslin would be a better buy than this low-count percale.

Sheet and pillowcase labels will also say if the fabric is "combed cotton". This means that it is woven of long, unbroken fibers, and it's another plus for wearability.

Social Security

How should Social Security benefits fit into my retirement plans?
Social Security benefits—which you build up during the years you work—give you a guaranteed monthly income after retirement, and also go part way in paying for increased medical expenses in old age. The income provided under Social Security is not enough to live on, plain and simple. However, it is a sound base for retirement planning, and you should always count on the basic pension payments under Social Security to help you meet your total retirement needs.

The amount of money you will receive

under Social Security depends on your average earnings over a period of years. This amount will change as your earnings increase or decrease from time to time throughout your working life. However, you can estimate the amount you are likely to receive at present rates, based on present earnings. You should make this estimate—and redo it periodically—so that you always have some idea of expected income under Social Security. Any local Social Security office will tell you what you will be due at age 62, or age 65 for your husband. If you want to figure it out for yourself, directions are contained in a booklet called *Your Social Security*. This booklet has other valuable information on Social Security. It costs 20 cents from the Superintendent of Documents, U.S. Government Printing Office, Washington, D.C. 20402. Ask for No. 1770-0193.

Can I get a rough idea of present Social Security payments?
Payments are based on average earnings, which are figured in a special way that is too complicated to go into here. For the sake of an example, however, let us say that a 65-year-old worker who is retiring today had average earnings of $5400. He will receive $250.60 per month in pension. If this retiree has a wife at least 62 years of age, she is also entitled to a monthly income. Their combined payment would be $344.60.

If this same couple's pension were figured on the husband's average earnings of $6600, the income would be $396.60, and on $7800, it would be $455.20.

I'm not sure that I won't want to work after I retire from my regular job, even if I don't need the money. How will working affect my Social Security benefits?
At the time of retirement, your Social Security office will explain to you exactly the then existing relationship between earnings and benefits. Right now the rule is:

If you earn $1680 or less in a year, you get full benefits.

If you earn more than $1680 a year, but less than $2880, your Social Security benefits will be reduced by $1 for each $2 of earnings.

If you earn more than $2880 a year, benefits are reduced dollar for dollar. The effect of this is to cancel out the benefits.

If you earn only $140 in any one month, you get full benefits for that month no matter what the total yearly earnings are. In other words, if earnings from January to June top $1680, your benefits will be reduced accordingly. However, if you earn only $120 per month from July to December, you will get full benefits for those months.

Keep in mind that nonearned income, such as interest and dividends, does not reduce Social Security benefits—no matter how high it might be. This should point up how important savings and investments are to financial security after retirement.

Is every person over 65 years of age protected by Social Security?
No, Social Security does not give blanket coverage to the elderly. Social Security only covers people who work for some part of their lives, whether as employees or as self-employed—and it is extended to wives of retired workers when they reach age 62.

In the early days of Social Security legislation, only 6 out of 10 workers were covered. Whole categories of workers, such as farmhands, domestics, and the self-employed, were excluded. Today, 9 out of 10 wage earners are building up Social Security benefits, and few categories are excluded.

To be fully insured under Social Security, a person must have worked a certain number of years. Depending on the year you reach age 65 (62 for women), you may be fully protected with credit for only $1\frac{1}{2}$ years of work. No one needs more than 10 years of work to qualify for monthly payments.

There are other Social Security benefits that protect the young as well as the elderly. These include payments to disabled children themselves, and to children of a worker who has become disabled, or who dies.

Financial assistance is also extended to a widow of any age if she is caring for a child. You will find clear explanations of most of the benefits under Social Security in the booklet, *Your Social Security*.

Medical Services

What is the difference between Medicare and Medicaid?
The two federal programs of Medicare and Medicaid are quite different. *Medicare* is the one especially for the elderly. It provides health insurance as an earned right to those who have paid into the program during their working years.

Medicaid is a federal health program for the poor of any age. Of course, because many of the poor are also elderly, it does help the aged in general to get better health care —but it depends on where they live. Medicaid is operated through the individual states by making federal funds available. States must match the funds offered by the national government, and not all states choose to do so. In fact, only about half the states have Medicaid programs, and they differ greatly in the benefits they give.

Each state sets the income limit for families they will assist under Medicaid. In some states, that income could be more than $4000 per year for a family of four. Information can be obtained from the State Welfare Department, or from the local office of the Department of Health, Education, and Welfare.

Does Medicare cover all elderly people?
To understand who is eligible for Medicare, you must first understand that Medicare has two parts to it: hospital insurance and medical insurance.

The *hospitalization* coverage is given automatically to all who come under Social Security (see page 137) or the Railroad Retirement Act. The *medical* insurance is a voluntary plan, open to anyone 65 or over. The government pays half-and-half with those who buy the plan so that the cost is one of the lowest for medical insurance.

My 72-year-old mother needs constant care, and we have been advised that she should be in a nursing home. Will Medicare help pay for this expense?
No, Medicare will not meet any expenses of nursing homes giving custodial care—that is, help in getting through the daily routine of bathing, dressing, eating, and moving about. Medicare will only pay for a necessary stay in a government-approved medical unit that may, in fact, be a nursing home. In this case, the Medicare patient must need special post-hospital care in connection with the same condition that caused hospitalization.

For such post-hospital care in a nursing home or like institution, Medicare covers up to 100 days. For the first 20 days, all specified expenses are met by the insurance. For the next 80 days, the patient must pay the first $8.50 of costs.

How much of the hospital bill does Medicare pay?
For the first 60 days of a hospital stay, Medicare pays everything over the first $68 of all covered services, which are fairly comprehensive. The patient's costs go up to $17 a day for the next 30 days. If a stay of longer than 90 days is necessary, the insured person can draw on a "lifetime reserve" of 60 additional days. However, costs go up again, and Medicare pays only after $34 a day is met by the patient.

Medicare payments are figured in benefit periods, and there is no limit on the number of benefit periods a person can have. When it comes to hospitalization for psychiatric reasons, however, Medicare has a lifetime limit of 190 days.

Please explain benefit period and lifetime reserve.
A benefit period, which is sometimes also called a spell of illness, goes from the day

you enter the hospital to the day you have been out of the hospital for 60 days running. For example, if you are in the hospital for 10 days, and out for 60, the benefit period is 70 days. If you return to the hospital even on the 71st day, a new benefit period starts.

The lifetime reserve comes to your aid if you need more than 90 days in the hospital during one benefit period. Each day used from this reserve is irreplaceable, and reduces the total number of reserve days due you. Thus, if you are in the hospital for 107 days, your lifetime reserve becomes 43 days—that is, the 17 days above 90 are subtracted from the 60-day reserve.

What does the voluntary medical plan of Medicare cover?

In general terms, the medical plan pays for 80 per cent of doctor bills and certain medical services over the first $50 of expenses in any one year. The doctor will be paid for his treatment in or out of the hospital, and some of the tests covered may be done in a hospital. Out-of-hospital psychiatric care is met up to $250 a year.

Is there any provision for home visits by nurses under Medicare?

Both the hospitalization and medical plans of Medicare provide for home care, and both cover up to 100 visits by nurses or other health workers. However, hospital insurance pays for home care only if it comes after, and is connected with, a hospital stay.

I have heard that it is cheaper to buy drugs by their generic name. What does this mean?

The generic name of drugs, like the generic name of anything else, is the common name given to all drugs of one kind. For example, aspirin is the generic name of one of the most commonly used nonprescription pain killers in the world. You can go into any drugstore and probably find aspirin at prices ranging from 29 to 89 cents for the same size of container. Similarly, *prednisone,* a drug now widely used in treating arthritis, costs six times more if bought by brand name rather than its generic name. Almost as startling is the fact that the often-prescribed antibiotic *tetracycline* costs one-half less under the generic name. Many tranquilizers run from one-fourth to one-third cheaper if you avoid buying them by their brand names.

Recently I asked my doctor to prescribe for me by generic name, but he gave me an argument. What am I to make of this?

Federal Drug Administration and Senate investigations have clearly proved that brand name drugs are more expensive—and, in some cases, outrageously higher—than the same drugs under their generic names. However, many doctors sincerely feel that there is more to it than price. They argue that there is better quality control by large companies producing drugs under a brand name. They feel, then, that brand name medicines are safer. In addition, hard-pressed doctors on busy schedules say it's hard to keep up with names of the many new drugs. The highly advertised brands stick in their minds and make it easier to prescribe.

Well-meant as these arguments may be, there is no proof that drugs made by small firms are inferior to brand name medicines in either quality or safety factors. In fact, some of the worst scandals on unsafe drugs have involved huge medical companies—usually when they release new drugs that have not been tested enough. Neither is it surprising that doctors remember brand names easier than generic names. Big pharmaceutical companies spend about $800 million a year in advertising directly to doctors—advertising that the general public isn't aware of.

You can't force your doctor to prescribe by generic name—and, of course, you shouldn't try if you trust him or her, and have a good relationship. However, you might talk the matter over again, and ask the doctor to consider the importance of the money savings to you.

Being a family with three young children, we are heavy users of vitamins. The expense is getting a bit ahead of us, but we feel that this health aid is important. How can we save on buying vitamins?

Many department stores, pharmacies, and discount houses sell vitamins under their own private brand. You will generally save a tidy sum if you buy these private brands instead of the famous trademarked names. (It's a similar story to generic v. brand name drugs.) You need be careful of only two things to make sure you are getting good value for money. First, look for the *U.S.P.* stamp on the label. U.S.P. stands for United States Pharmaceutical Association, and its stamp means that the product meets certain standards of quality. Second, check on the potency of the vitamins, and be sure they are of the strength you need.

You can also save a good deal of money by getting your vitamins from a low-cost mail-order firm. Of course, you must plan ahead so that you don't run out of your supply before the next order arrives. If you buy by mail, it is possible to pay about 30 to 50 per cent less than regular retail prices.

Two well-known mail-order houses of sound reputation are: Hudson Vitamin Products, 89 Seventh Ave., New York, N.Y. 10001, and Direct Drug Service, 823 Upshur Street N.W., Washington, D.C. 20011.

Home Improvement Rackets

I read a newspaper story about a woman getting fleeced through the "referral racket", but the story wasn't very clear on how the racket works. Can you tell me how to avoid getting caught myself?

The referral racket is one of the common swindles involving home improvements. Swindlers are usually extremely successful because they work it on big, one-time jobs—then disappear before the victim can do anything. Here is what generally happens.

A man turns up at your door selling aluminum siding—or expensive wall-to-wall carpeting, or a paint job, or an added-on room. He tells you the improvement will cost you nothing because he will use your home as a showplace, and pay you $25 each time he brings someone to see it. He may also offer a cash bonus if you yourself get orders for the same improvement.

If you fall for this—and, remember, these salesmen are not only aggressively persistent, but also golden-tongued in double talk—you will sign a contract for, say, the aluminum siding. After the job is done, you wait endlessly and hopelessly for the masses of referrals the con man promised. None come. But your bills for the work do, and you have to pay. If you do get someone else interested in having the work done so that you can earn the promised commission, you can't find the man who did the work. (The company with whom you signed the contract is seldom at the address listed.)

Besides the aggravation and expense, you will probably also discover that the work and product were inferior. You're stuck—like thousands of other homeowners who are bilked of millions every year by the referral and other home improvement rackets.

Your best protection against such frauds? Close the door in the face of any door-to-door contractor—or hang up the phone if the contact is made that way. John L. Springer, author of *Consumer Swindlers and How to Avoid Them*, says: "My investigations convinced me that fully 75 per cent of home improvement gyps are started with a ringing phone or doorbell." So, slam the door or bang down the receiver without regret for what you may feel is rudeness. It may save you from a giant gyp.

What are some other home improve-

ment gyps I should know about and guard against?

Another of the frequent fakers who might turn up at your door is the furnace repairman. He might say he is a government inspector, and flash an identification card at you. If he uses this official inspector dodge, he may either offer to do the job himself, or recommend a repairman who will call on you in the next few hours. Or, he might just sweeten you with a story that he can do repairs cheaper because "I work from my truck, so I have no overhead." In any case, once he has gained access to your cellar, your furnace has had it. With a scare story of some sort—perhaps that the furnace might actually blow up—he'll likely take the equipment apart and scatter the pieces all over the floor. At that point, you can't do much except let him put it back together again. He does. You not only have to pay a price that's way out of line, but you may also end up with a second repair bill to right what he's done wrong.

Still another favorite fraud of the home improvement sharks is the roof repair job. This could start with your opening the door to a person who is acting the "concerned citizen". He may say he's noticed a dangerous sag in your roof, and wants to inform you out of concern. Before long, this concerned citizen turns himself into a skilled craftsman, and you find yourself signing up for major roof work to be done by him. There are records showing that such jobs have run to $1500 or so. Often, they were not needed at all. Sometimes, although necessary, they could have been done for about half the cost by reputable roofers.

What should I do about the furnace or roofer type of trickster?

These two racketeers point up several more "don'ts" for the homeowner who doesn't want to be hoodwinked. First, don't be taken in by a claim that someone is a government inspector if he does anything more than inspect. Government employees are not allowed to try to sell you something, nor can they speak in favor of one particular product or firm. Ask to examine a so-called inspector's identification, and do so carefully. Even better, phone the agency he claims to work for to find out if he is, in fact, employed there. Guaranteed he won't still be at the door when you get back from the phone call.

Second, don't take the first price anyone quotes you for any home improvements. Get bids from several local companies. In addition, ask the companies making bids to let you see some of their finished work, or to give you the names of satisfied customers with whom you can talk. It's always the better part of wisdom to check with the Better Business Bureau about a company's business record.

Finally, don't let the job be started without a written contract—but one that you understand completely. Be sure it sets out the work to be done, the rate to be charged, the brand names or grades of material to be used, and the date on which the work is to be completed.

If it seems like you have to be on your toes every minute to avoid the con artists in the home improvement field, that's exactly right. The racketeers are geniuses of the gyp, and keep coming up with variations on the old themes. They don't deserve a penny of your money. Don't give them one.

Repairs Rackets

I know that TV sets are complicated, but do all repair charges have to be so high that I feel cheated every time?

In answer to your first point, TV sets are not all that complicated when it comes to most repairs. Consumer researchers have found that, most of the time, TV troubles are caused by a faulty vacuum tube. It is simply a matter of finding and replacing the tube that's not working. Yet, your complaint about high charges is a common one. This is because TV repairmen frequently make unnecessary repairs just to hike the price, or charge skyhigh for labor on simple repairs like tube replacements. It has also been found that some TV repair services use old parts so that the set will have another breakdown soon after one servicing.

There are a couple of good ways to fight TV swindles. First of all, it is entirely possible for you, as a layman, to learn enough about the TV tubes to find and replace faulty ones yourself. Just use a good instruction book to help you locate the various tubes, take several to an electrical shop to test them, and replace any that are bad. A highly recommended book on TV do-it-yourself is *Make Your Own TV Repairs* by Art Margolis. It is put out by Arco Publications, and, if you can't borrow it from your local library, it might be worth buying at $3.50.

Next, be prepared against the serviceman who says your TV set must be taken away to his shop for what he calls a bench test. In such a case, insist on getting an estimate in writing first. If he says he can't do that without testing the set further, make him sign a statement that he will not start any work until he has sent you an estimate, and you have said to go ahead.

Nothing infuriates me more than the gouging prices of auto repairs, especially when I'm almost sure that half the work done is totally unnecessary. What can I do about it, short of becoming a car mechanic myself?
There are several safeguards that will help you protect yourself against the widespread and frequent shady dealings of auto repair services. These are the suggestions of writers and workers in the field of consumer protection.

One way to avoid overpaying for auto repairs is to deal with one, and only one, garage or service station. Buy all your gas and oil, and get all your servicing done there. Use the same place for body-and-fender work if possible, or ask the owner for his recommendation. He may have a tie-in with a body-and-fender shop, which will make him pleased to get still more business from you. In other words, make yourself such a good customer that your garage won't want to lose your business. Not only are you likely to get better service, but you are also unlikely ever to be tricked.

Another protective measure is to get a written estimate on major repairs, even if you are dealing with your regular garage. In fact, it's wisest to get two or three different estimates. Tell whichever serviceman you decide on to let you know if he finds that additional work has to be done after he starts on the repairs mentioned in the estimate. In this way, you are less likely to get the shock of a whopping bill for unexpected repairs you didn't ask to be done.

Even for minor repairs, it's a good idea to get an oral estimate from more than one auto repair shop.

My car was heavily damaged in a collision, and, even though it was my first accident, I had a rough time collecting repair costs from my insurance company. This hardly seems fair, but what's to be done?
The tough attitude taken by insurance companies even on legitimate claims may have to be resolved by protective legislation for the consumer eventually. Meantime, it always makes things easier if you give your insurance representative a written estimate from your garage before going ahead with the needed repairs. If you don't clear with the insurance company in this way, you might have an expensive fight to collect.

Sales Gimmicks

I never heard of the "bait-and-switch" gimmick until I got hooked by it. Can you explain this dirty selling trick to others so they won't fall for it as I did?
Bait-and-switch selling is a commonplace

danger to the consumer. It is tried with television sets, washing machines, furniture suites, carpeting, automobiles, and many other products. It is tried in every season, and in most places—and it succeeds so much of the time that one wonders how so many shoppers can allow themselves to be fooled.

Here's how it works. Suppose you've been looking for an air conditioner, and have done enough comparison shopping and study to know what is good value. One day you see an ad for the kind of air conditioner you want, at a price that is quoted as "below wholesale." You should be suspicious immediately, because no retailer can stay long in business if he doesn't charge enough to meet his rent, payroll, and other normal expenses. But, you don't think of that. (We hope you will in the future.) You know from your research that the price is, indeed, low, and you hurry to the shop to make your grand killing.

Once in the shop, you are told that all the advertised air conditioners have been sold. (You should know from now on that, no matter how early you turn up, all the advertised merchandise will be gone.) However, the glib salesman has another, even better model to offer—though, of course, it is higher priced. You're there, you're tired of rushing off to hunt bargains, the salesman is a hard pusher, and you buy. Result? You've spent a great deal more than you wanted to, and, perhaps, more than the product you got is worth.

There are numerous variations of the bait-and-switch swindle. For example, the advertised merchandise may be on display, but it will be an old model or a damaged piece. The salesman switches your attention to a more expensive item even before you muster your outrage at the fact that the ad was deceiving. Sometimes there is no newspaper ad at all, and the merchandise for sale is featured in a window. Then the dodge usually is that the window display is the last of its kind in the whole store, and cannot be removed.

On large purchases, such as funiture or carpeting, you may find yourself manouvered into signing a contract for hundreds of dollars. It's all part of the bait-and-switch racket, and the earlier warning about not signing contracts holds here if you want to avoid trouble.

A few weeks ago I received a language lesson record in the mail. I had not ordered it, and didn't feel like tramping to the post office to send it back, so it's just lying around. However, the firm that sent it is dunning me for payment. What are my rights in the matter?

You are under no legal obligation either to pay for mailed merchandise you didn't order, or to mail it back. The con men who do this kind of thing hope you will think you have to pay if you keep whatever they send. They know most people don't go to the bother of rewrapping a package, and carting it to the post office to return it. So they figure you'll take the easier way of sending the couple of dollars in payment. Don't be duped.

Since 1970 a federal law decrees that if you receive unordered merchandise, you need not pay for it, nor return it. That, in effect, says you can keep whatever you get in the mail, and ignore all threats from the sender about nonpayment. Some states have gone a step further, and have laws under which all unordered merchandise is considered as a gift from the sender—no strings attached. Neither the FTC nor the state laws have solved the problem of dunning letters—but you can solve that very easily yourself by tossing them into the wastebasket without even opening them, and forgetting about them.

Sometimes the sender of unordered merchandise is a charity. This may put a psychological pressure on you to pay—perhaps out of guilt or a sense of responsibility. However, the unfairness of this selling technique is the same whether the seller is a commercial or charitable organization. Protect yourself accordingly.

For Your Bookshelf

Family Guide to Financial Security
Rutledge Books, Inc. and The Benjamin Co., Inc. (New York: 1972)

Your Social Security
U.S. Government Printing Office (Washington D.C.: 1972)

Getting The Most for Your Money
by Anthony Scaduto, Paperback Library (New York: 1971)

Make Your Own TV Repairs
by Art Margolis, Arco Publishing Co. (New York: 1968)

The Consumer's Guide to Better Buying
by Sidney Margolius, Pocket Books (New York: 1972)

The Money Tree
by Catherine Crook de Camp, Signet Books (New York: 1972)

How to Buy Stocks
by Louis Engel, Bantam Books, Inc. (New York: 1972)

Consumer Reports Buying Guide 1973
Consumers Union of United States, Inc. (Mount Vernon, N.Y.: 1972)

Picture Credits

© Aldus Books (Photos Mike Busselle) 11(TL), 15(BR), 16, 21(BR), 28, 38(T), 46, 53, 55, 57, 63, 79(R), 108, 110, 112; (courtesy Espley & Espley Advertising) 4, 58-59; (courtesy Liden Products (Whitewood) Ltd.) 61(T); Artist Mary Tomlin 31-33, 37, 41-43, 65, 71-73, 77, 80-81, 86-87, 98-101, 124; Aldus Archives, Cover CB; after *Personal Money Management,* American Banks Association, Washington, D.C. 74(B); after *How to Get the Most for Your Food Dollar,* Award Books, New York, 1970 37; Bibliothèque Nationale, Paris 9(T); British Crown Copyright 10(BR); Reproduced by permission of the Trustees of the British Museum 8(T), (Photo © Aldus Books) 9(BL), (Photo John Webb © Aldus Books) 6(BL); Camera Press/Barnet Staidman 9(BR); J. Allan Cash 89(T); after *Changing Times,* March, 1970 111; The Chase Manhattan Bank, New York 10(T); Reproduced from a painting by Roger Coleman 13(TR); Colorific! (Jim Pickerau) 7(TR)(BR), (Don Humptien) 122, (John Moss) 127; after information from The Conference Board, New York, 19(B); *Daily Telegraph* Colour Library 11(CR); C. M. Dixon, London, 15(TR); after *How to Stretch Your Dollar,* Fawcett World Library, New York, 1971 65; Courtesy Board of Governors of the Federal Reserve System, Washington, D.C. 25(T), 50(L); Graham Finlayson 7(BL); First National City Corporation 11(TR), 22-23, 25(B), 44, 52; Fox Photos 94(B); FPG Cover BL, R, 38(B), 67, 68(L), 92(B), 93(T), 96(L), 104, (Hallinan) 2, 20(TR) (B), 21(BL) 26, 34-35, 39, 69(B), 85, 116. (Houfman) 15(BL), (Joh Gajda) 20(TL), (Jerrold Cohen) 20(2nd from TR), (H. Spival 21(TL)(TR). (Lee Langum) 51, (C. Smith) 60, (Georg Schwartz) 62(L), (Sandak) 89(B), (F. Miller) 92(TL), (Timmerson) 93(B), 97, (Hal McKusick) 105(T), 118(TL), (Ejey) 105(B), (J. Baker) 113, 114(L), (Bea Perran) 115, (R. Slater) 119, (Hal Yaeger) 123; Gamma (Rene Maestri) 13(BR), (Burk Uzzle) 75, 78; By courtesy of Stanley Gibbons Ltd. 12(BR); Georg Gerster/The John Hillelson Agency Ltd. 95; Michael Holford Library photos 8(BR), 13(BL); Mansell Collection 6(T), 8(BL); Paul Berman/Marshall Cavendish 106; after *Your Housing Dollar,* Money Management Institute, Chicago 102; Musée Municipal, Menton/Photo Giraudon 10(BL); The National Gallery, London Cover TL, 14(T); after information from National Live Stock and Meat Board, Chicago 31; *Paris Match* 12(T); Picturepoint, London 7(TL), 14(B), 84, 91; Private Collection, England 12(BL); after information from Survey Research Center, The University of Michigan 47, 48; Carlton Smith and Richard Putnam Pratt, *The Time-Life Book of Family Finance,* Time-Life Inc., New York, 1969 24, 49, 109(R); Transworld *(American Home)* 30, 66(L), 69(R), 90, *(Family Circle)* 18(B), 19(T), 83, 121, (John Launois) 117(R); after information from U.S. Bureau of Labor Statistics, Washington, D.C. 29; after information from U.S. Department of Commerce 103; after *Statistical Abstract of the United States,* U.S. Department of Commerce, Washington, D.C. 1972 74(TL); Wells Fargo Bank N.A. 11 (BR)